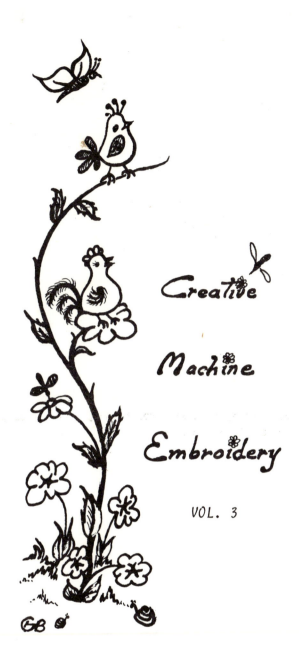

Creative Machine Embroidery

VOL. 3

by

Lucille Merrell Graham

To my Mother. She left me many wonderful gifts, and the one I
enjoy most is the Gift of Creativity.

Acknowledgments

To my husband who has helped so much in making the manuscript concise, and has taken a great share of my daily tasks, leaving my time free to work on *The Book*.

Apologies to my family for neglecting—yes, even ignoring them at times while the work was in progress.

Dear LuRae Barlow was always available to give an opinion or lend a hand in any way I needed. She has contributed several items for the book, and has helped in so many ways.

Thanks to Linda Goff, that lovely and competent gal who has taken over my teaching joys. It is exciting to see her expand on my methods, and I'm so pleased to have her chapter on *Cutwork* in this book.

Our able and clever artists who did most of the designs for embroidery are Gail Brown and Ann Haskett.

Gayle Bailey, a professional typist and a great *second miler*, took my rag-tag manuscript and made these tidy pages.

And just to add another *Gail*, we were lucky enough to get Gail Hartman working on the photography, also that thoughtful and kind Bill Sugden.

To all who have assisted, encouraged, and prodded, *Thanks*.

Introduction

At last we have color in our book—something you have been requesting for a long time. And all new designs, each prepared as a hot iron transfer in the pattern packet at the back of the book.

Each design has been worked up onto an appropriate item and is pictured in full color in the center section. Each item has instruction given, with pictures and illustrations, also suggestions for other uses of the design.

A number of items in the book are embroidered on printed fabric. No patterns are given of course, but instructions and ideas for doing these and similar things of your own are there.

An important feature of this book is the *Stitch Glossaries,* one for Embroidery and one for Yarn Stitchery. This should be invaluable for beginners and a nice review for those with experience.

Many of the techniques given appear in unexpected or obscure places, so you'd better read every word! If you see something you may want to refer to later, make a note in the margin or dog-ear the page.

Rules and tradition have no place in Machine Embroidery. We give you instructions to help you learn the basic techniques, and urge you to explore the vast possibilities for expressing yourself creatively.

Although this book was written with the experienced embroiderer in mind, the basics are given clearly enough for those who are just beginning. It is hoped that all will find it interesting and beneficial.

We should tell you that Volumes 1 and 2 of *Creative Machine Embroidery* are alive and doing well. (See *Sources.*) You will find these filled with exciting ideas, designs and techniques, with detailed instruction for each.

It is hoped that you will find great joy and satisfaction of creative expression in the use of your machine for embroidery.

Table of Contents

Floral Afghan   Instructions pages 125–129

Understand Your Machine

Every machine runs better with proper cleaning and oiling. Consult your sewing machine manual for help on this, or Volumes 1 or 2 of *Creative Machine Embroidery*.

To know how your machine works, tip the head back and watch as it makes a stitch. Turn the flywheel slowly by hand and see the threaded needle come down through the opening in the needle plate. As it descends the hook is moving around the bobbin case. The needle starts upward, leaving a loop of thread to be picked up by the hook. This loop is carried half way around the bobbin case and then released. Meanwhile the needle is rising and the take-up lever is pulling the loop taut around the bobbin thread, forming a stitch on the fabric.

The relationship between the eye of the needle and the action of the hook is referred to as *timing* of the machine.

In order to form the stitches, the material must be held firmly against the needle plate. This is the function of the presser foot and feed dogs. For free embroidery we remove the presser foot and lower or cover the feed dogs, thus losing that advantage. In order to compensate, the material being embroidered must be held taut and pressed against the needle plate while the stitches are forming. This is done by placing the fabric in a hoop or holding it with the hands, the hoop being the better.

With some machines, and on many occasions with *all* machines, we need extra help with holding the material firmly for the stitches to form, and we get this with the use of the darning foot which comes with many machines, or with a darning spring.

This darning foot is the one which hops up and down as the needle raises and lowers. On some machines this foot is just a thin circle and works well for embroidery. On others it is bulky and blocks the view of the needle as it enters the fabric. A handyman can clip off the front of this foot, leaving a horseshoe shape open at the front, making it quite satisfactory.

The *darning spring* works well on all machines. (See *Sources*.) This little spring slips up onto the needle and has a wire at the top which is bent over the needle clamp screw to hold it securely in place.

A word of explanation about these springs—some are long and slender, requiring that you remove them each time the needle is threaded, others are more wide and squatty, allowing you to easily slip the thread down through, or even take the thread out around it and into the needle.

Problems and Solutions

Thread Breaking:

Think first of the needle. It must be sharp, straight, and in the machine correctly. Even a slight injury to the needle can dull or bend it enough to cause problems. Try a new one anyway to see if it helps. The flat side of the needle shank is always placed next to the machine.

Incorrect tensions cause thread breakage. See chapter *Understand Your Machine* for help on this.

Using a spring on the needle is sometimes all the help you need in preventing broken threads.

If the fabric is not kept taut in the hoop, the thread will sometimes break. If your hoop is inadequate, try wrapping the inner ring with gauze bandage to hold the fabric firmly.

A small rough spot on the bobbin case or needle plate can snag the thread and break it. Try smoothing this with emery cloth or board, and see a service man if it needs more help.

If bobbin thread breaks, check for rough spots.

If none of these things seem to apply, you may have a timing problem with your machine and you should take it to a service man.

Skipping Stitches:

Same as above.

Puckers:

The reason for puckers is that there is more pull on the thread than resistance on the material. Therefore, we must find the proper balance.

The fabric *must* be held taut even if it requires wrapping the hoop or buying a new one.

Tensions too tight will pucker the fabric every time. You must really work to understand the tensions on your own machine, then this will never need be a problem for you.

Paper under your work will prevent puckering, and it must be stiff enough to resist the pull of the zig zag stitch. Iron on facing works the same way.

Proper needle size is important. A large needle will cause pucker every time. The finest needle that will carry the thread you are using is best for embroidery.

A narrow stitch is less apt to pucker than a wide one, and a straight stitch is best of all for this.

Needles Break:

The best cure for this is Patience. Free embroidery is so different from work we do with the presser foot, and it takes time and experience to get the feel of this. Just remember to run the machine fast and move your hands slowly. Keep your motions smooth and gentle, and you will overcome.

Heating of Motor and Control:

Heating is caused by running too slowly or by a machine that is sluggish in action, usually due to inadequate cleaning and lubrication of the machine. Continued use of oil other than specified sewing machine oil can also cause sluggishness by gumming up the moving parts.

It is normal for the control to heat up during sustained operation, especially when running slowly. The motor will tolerate moderate heating, the control will withstand considerably more. Put something under it to protect the carpet.

The smell of over-heating is an indication that it has reached its limit. To cool the motor quickly, disengage the flywheel as if you were going to wind a bobbin, then run the machine at full speed for a minute or two. This will remove the peak of heat from the motor, allowing it to cool much faster as it rests awhile.

Fabric too Small for Hoop:

You could no doubt embroider the small item by holding it taut with your fingers, but you would have more freedom for doing good work if it were stretched in a hoop. Simply machine baste strips of scrap material to the edges and make it large enough for the hoop.

Feed Dogs in Constant Action:

Some machines have no way of lowering or covering the feed dogs for doing embroidery work, thus making smooth embroidery difficult. Consider removing the feed dogs by taking out a couple of screws. Check with your service man to see if this is advisable.

Necessary Equipment

Machine:
Of first importance is a freshly cleaned and oiled machine. Any home style zig zag machine in good running order should be able to do this work.

The following items may be difficult to find in your area. If so, mail order suppliers are listed in the back of the book.

Embroidery Hoops:
Use those made specifically for the sewing machine, as they are shallow for ease in slipping under the needle and presser bar. These also have a screw for tightening. Popular are the 4, 6, 8, and 10 inch sizes. The eight inch is probably the most versatile, but you will likely want all of them eventually.

Machine Embroidery Thread:
See *Threads* for full coverage of this.

Needles:
Use the finest needle that will carry the thread you are using; #11 or #70 is an excellent choice for most embroidery work.

Darning Foot or Spring:
This is described fully in *Understand Your Machine.*

Fabrics:
We refuse to make any rules about which fabrics work best because we are convinced that *all* fabrics may be satisfactorily embroidered on the machine if one has the determination to do it.

In general, a firmly woven cotton or rayon, or a combination of the two in a linen-like weave works very well for embroidering samplers, pictures, etc. Heavy, firm linen is excellent too. But please do not limit yourself in any way to choosing favorites. Try everything, and enjoy them all!

In the chapter on *Embroidering the Clothing You Make,* the merits and the limitations of many fabrics are discussed, and you will no doubt find this helpful. Also, in *Embroider a Knit* you will find thorough discussion which is most helpful.

Transferring the Design

Patterns:
The simplest designs to use are the hot iron transfer patterns such as those in the packet at the back of this book, or those sold in the stores.

The patterns given here are of the slow-transfer ink type which stamp off several times, as opposed to the quick transfer wax type which stamp only once.

To use our patterns, turn the iron to the setting for the fabric you are using. Position the design inked side down on the fabric and press with the hot iron. Plan on at least half a minute for the design to develop, then peek under the edge to check for brightness of transfer. Give it all the time it needs.

Make a Transfer Pattern:
To make your own transfer designs, use a *hot iron transfer pencil,* (See *Sources*) and simply trace your design onto tissue paper. For monograms or other places where direction of design is important, trace the *wrong* side of the design with the transfer pencil so that it will be the correct direction when ironed on.

Art Tracing Paper Method:
We specify art tracing paper because it is the best we have found for this method. However, any transparent brittle paper such as thin onion skin will do.

This method is used when the color or fiber of your fabric prevents you from using the hot iron method. It is also ideal for hard to reach places.

Trace your design onto the paper. Pin in place on the fabric and put it under the needle. You will probably want to use the hoop for this.

Using thread to match the fabric or design you plan to embroider, go over all of the lines with a straight stitch, moving slowly so that the paper will break away readily when you are through.

When all of the lines are stitched, remove the paper by gently stretching the fabric on the bias to help it break away from the stitching. With the paper all off, your design is ready to be embroidered.

Organdy Transfer:
A really good method of transferring is to trace the design onto organdy or other thin, crisp fabric. Pin in place and with a Liquid Embroidery Pen or Permanent Felt Tip Pen, go over all the lines, letting the pen marks penetrate the organdy and put the design onto the fabric to be embroidered.

Threads

Most machines respond best to specified Machine Embroidery Thread, and for this reason we recommend that beginners use only this type. Once you have the feel of this work and know how your machine responds, try any and all threads. There's great excitement in discovering the many varieties and the effects they may produce.

Machine Embroidery Thread is at present marketed by several different companies and more are appearing as the popularity of this art spreads. Find the market in your locality, and be on the lookout for new products. Mail order sources for thread are listed in the back.

Thread Fibers:
Cotton machine embroidery thread is the most readily available. This is lustrous and smooth, giving a lovely sheen to your work, and it is easy to use.

Rayon thread is found in the stores in some areas, and we hope it will soon be everywhere. It is rather coarse, very shiny, and spectacular results are possible when using it. Being slippery, it tends to slide from the upright spool and can be frustrating to use. However, a device called a *Thread Tree* has recently come into our hands and this solves the problem. It holds the spool horizontally, letting the thread pull off evenly with hardly ever a tangle. For the address see *Sources*.

Cotton thread is available in sizes 30, 50, and 60, the lower numbers being the heavier weights.

Size 30 being rather coarse, it gives a beautiful texture and is great for heavy fill-in and fast buildup, especially on larger areas. However, special care must be taken to keep the stitches going in the right direction, as a crosswise stitch is usually obvious in this heavier thread. This size is ideal for broad monogram lines, and for working on vinyl and heavy fabrics — difficult for fine detail work and on delicate fabrics.

Some machines require the strength of this heavier thread for success in embroidering.

Size 50 can be depended on for most uses. Delicate enough for the finest work, yet adequate for most heavy embroidery, it is the most versatile size of all.

Size 60 is still finer, and excellent for the most intricate and delicate work — inadequate for heavy fill-in, or embroidering large areas.

Yardage per spool is important, affecting cost and convenience. When comparing, remember that a heavy thread covers more area per yard than does a fine one.

In purchasing your first thread, you may obtain a greater variety of colors for the money invested in buying the low yardage spools. These will be practical also for the colors you use infrequently. For the colors you use most often the larger spools would be more convenient. Those of us who do a great deal of embroidery need large quantities of all the threads.

Experiment to see which threads work best for you and then obtain all you can afford. The greatest variety of materials available will give you the best advantage for being creative.

Metallic thread is usually not made of metal, but is bright and shiny as metal would be. It is usually resistant to tarnishing and remains lustrous through endless laundering.

This thread comes in gold and silver and fills its role mainly in small areas of accent. Consider using it for the veins of a leaf, a flower center, to add a touch of shine on a monogram, or to highlight an embroidered eye.

Many companies are making these metallic threads. Most are designed for handwork and very few are adaptable for use on the machine. See *Sources* for the one you can count on.

Stitches—a Glossary

There are actually only three basic machine embroidery stitches: straight stitch, satin stitch, and side stitch. Everything we do is a variation or combination of these.

Let us picture how the machine makes these stitches. In doing a straight stitch, the needle simply goes up and down, punching holes to form stitches. The way we move the material with our hands determines the direction the stitches will go.

If we set the machine for a zig zag the needle swings from side to side parallel to the front of the machine. The type of embroidery we do with the zig zag is determined by the direction we move the material under the swing of the needle, and the angle at which the material is lying when the stitches are formed.

Straight Stitch:
　　Set the machine for straight stitch and simply slide the material wherever you want the stitches to go with no worry about rotating the hoop. This stitch is used a great deal for small details, accenting of embroidered areas, *filler* stitches, contouring, and much more.

Satin Stitch:
　　This is done by letting the needle swing from side to side across the line as shown in the illustration. The zig zag may be any width from the finest to the widest your machine will make. The material should be moved slowly so that the stitches are closely packed. Move freely forward, backward, or wherever you desire.

Side Stitch:
　　This doesn't look like much by itself, but then it is seldom used alone. Make this stitch by positioning the material in such a way that the needle swings the same direction you want the stitching to go, then moving the material sideways so that the stitching is traced in that direction.

On the following pages will be found stitched illustrations and instructions for using these stitches singly, and in combination. This is by no means complete, as there is no end to the interesting innovations possible.

Stitch Variations

Straight Stitch Uses

Fine Detail:
    Fine thread and straight stitch are a must for work this fine. It is really quite easy to do, as you have better control when using a straight stitch than a zig zag. Simply slide the material so that the needle traces the lines.

Accenting:
    The two flowers were embroidered exactly alike except for the accenting. Accent stitching always makes a great difference in your finished embroidery.

    To do this, a straight stitch is used, and thread of a dark, sharp shade of appropriate color. The jagged effect is achieved by moving in and out very slightly along the petal edges, going deeper at the indentations. The amount of stitching you apply determines the heaviness of the accent.

    If you wish a smooth line of accent around an embroidered object, simply put a row of straight stitch around it as was done with the cherries. However, a single line of straight stitch sometimes appears a bit stringy and is improved by going over it again.

Filler Stitches:
    These are most often done with straight stitch, and are used to *fill* an area where you want an embroidered effect without a great deal of stitching.

    The filler in the leaf is just a series of out-and-back lines, giving the appearance of veins.

    For the cherry an open, no-grainline effect is desirable, and this calls for a *squiggle* stitch. To do this simply move the material under the needle in a random manner, making a continuous serpentine line of straight stitches.

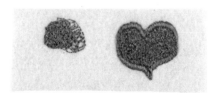

Solid Filler:
    You may use a straight stitch for this when a fine texture is desired, or a zig zag for heavier texture.

9

The stitch is made by moving the material rapidly in a tight circular motion, overlapping circles until the fabric is entirely covered with thread.

Use this whenever you wish a *no-grainline* effect such as on faces or other skin areas, flower centers, hearts, etc.

Straight Stitch for Contours:
    Accurate contouring is much easier with straight stitch than with zig zag. As the needle goes straight up and down there is no worry about turning the material for proper grainline. Simply slide it to let the needle trace a line or fill an area. If you pretend that the needle is a pencil and make it trace the lines of a curve or fill a curved area as you would with a pencil or crayon, it soon becomes easy. Use this in shaping fruits, flowers, leaves, or anywhere you wish.

A fun trick in doing this apple was using two shades of thread at once. This helps to define the curves, and it makes the color more realistic.

Satin Stitch Uses

Curves:
    Satin stitch straight lines were illustrated two pages back. From straight lines to curved lines is but a simple step. Just slide the material where you want to go and let the needle trace the line. Do not turn the material to follow the curve, but simply slide it. It may help if you pretend that the needle is a pencil and move the material under it in such a way that it traces whatever shape you wish to make. Practice all sorts of curving lines, especially writing.

Tip—When moving forward or backward, move slowly for a well packed satin stitch. When going sideways on the curve, move more quickly to avoid awkward overlap of stitches.

Circles:
    Circles are no more difficult than are curves. Simply keep going to close the line all the way around. The heaviness of the circle will be determined by the width of the zig zag used.

Writing:

From making circles it is an easy
step to writing. An interesting thing
shows up in this illustration. For
small lettering you need small stitches.
The first three letters look fine, but
the last two are almost blotted out by
the wide stitching. Wider widths
should be saved for larger writing.

In our home we have *The Lord's
Prayer* and *The 23rd Psalm* which I
embroidered (See Vol. 2 page 55).
Many who see these marvel that I could
do this fine printing with the machine.
A nice boost for the ego, but undeserved.
Fine stitching is no more difficult than
any other, as writing with a fine pen is
just as easy as with a heavy point.

By the way, if you sign your work
with a straight stitch, your signature
may get more raves than the embroidered
piece.

Serpentine:

This is just an extension of the
squiggle stitch, made by moving the
material to form a random design using
satin stitch width of your choice. As
a filler this stitch cannot be beat.

Use serpentine to fill a leaf,
flower, monogram, or any area you wish.
It can stand alone, as shown in the
flower heads of the Yucca in *Hills of
Home* in the color section. You may fill
a piece of fabric with this stitch to
use as part of a pattern in clothing
construction such as collar, cuffs,
yoke, sleeves, pockets, panel, belt, etc.

French Knots:

French knots are made simply by piling up a few satin stitches. The width of the stitch determines the size of the knot, the number of stitches determines the depth. There are so many uses for these knots, and such varied ways of making them that we must explore a few.

Of the five clusters shown here, the top one is made with #1 zig zag, the second one with #2, third with #3, and fourth with #4. The lower cluster shows one very large knot made with #4 width stitched very heavily. A circle of a darker shade of thread surrounds it, with a ring of tiny knots in the same dark shade.

Tip—When making large French knots, fasten the thread after each one by making a few straight stitches close to the edge.

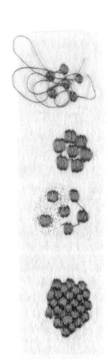

This cluster of French knots shows each one accurately placed, with a length of thread pulled up between each to assist in clipping the threads closely.

The next cluster shows larger knots closer together with no clipping of threads needed. To avoid surplus thread between knots, finish each one with the last stitch close to where the next knot will be, then proceed from one knot to another in that manner.

In making a flower center with filled in background and French knots, do the knots first with no worry about threads in between. Do the fill-in afterwards, covering the lengths of thread at that time.

Realistic berries may be made using medium French knots placed close together in a random way so that the *bumps* appear as berry seeds.

Directional Tapering:
     Look at the stylized leaf. The embroidered lines are tapered from thick to thin in several places.

     Where there is a curving line it is fairly easy to get this tapered effect. A few practice leaves would be helpful in discovering how best to position the stitches. This leaf was placed with the needle swinging sideways at both pointed tips. Using the widest zig zag and holding the material at the same angle for the entire outline, the curvy thick-and-thin lines were made.

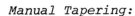

Manual Tapering:
     This is a bit tricky, but worth all the practice it requires. The principle here is to widen and narrow the zig zag by controlling the lever with your right hand, and slowly moving the material with the left hand.

     The first key to success is the mechanical control of the zig zag on your machine. It should move freely so that you can widen and narrow the stitch smoothly. If the lever on your machine drops into notches as you move it across, more muscle power and coordination are required.

     Begin your practice with a few little *lazy daisy* leaves. Starting at the stem, run a line of straight stitches to the top of the first leaf. Place index finger and middle finger at either side of the line and move the material slowly away from you while the right hand widens and narrows the stitch.

     Now with straight stitch trace the stem to the next leaf, then out to the tip, and repeat the widening and narrowing process. Practice this as much as it takes to achieve a freedom of motion, then use it with confidence.

     Tapering long lines is just an extension of the lazy daisy. Play around with shapes such as these leaves and see what you can do. This sort of *doodling* will pay big dividends in better coordination of the hands and machine, and should be indulged in often.

Side Stitch Uses:

Before learning how to use it, let's be sure we know how to *do* it. If you move the material sideways as the stitches are forming, you are making a side stitch. Moving forward or backward makes a satin stitch.

Look closely at these two leaves. The upper one is side stitched. The leaf was lying on its side in front of me and I was sliding it sideways as it was embroidered.

The lower leaf is satin stitched. The end of the leaf was pointing toward me and I moved it forward and backward for the embroidery.

Notice that the side stitched leaf is more slender appearing with sharply pointed points. The satin stitched leaf has blunt points. Each technique gives a lovely appearance and may be used separately or combined.

On this leaf each of the sections was done with side stitch. Each section was lying on its side for embroidery and the material moved sideways to make graceful lines and sharp points.

Side stitch can usually be counted on for graceful detail lines such as leaf veins and accents on petals. A relaxed approach to this type of detail will produce a more natural appearance.

For the vein structure on the rose leaf, the leaf was lying on its side. Beginning at the base of the leaf and using a narrow zig zag, each pair of veins was done with an out-and-back motion, ending up at the top. The center vein was then re-stitched to the lower edge, and the stitching extended to include the stem.

The vein structure of the oak leaf above was done in much the same way with the needle swinging sideways on each of the sections.

14

Feather Stitch:

This is useful and lovely for leaves, fuzzy animals, ducks, chicks, etc.

To do this leaf, set a medium-to-wide zig zag and work sideways across the outline. Move in and out in a random manner, making uneven lines of stitching. The material should be rotated as you work to keep the stitch moving sideways at all times. If you fail to do this, blunt, heavy lines of stitching will occur, and it will not look feathery at all!

The little dog is from a commercial iron-on design, and was embroidered as stamped. Stitching was narrow (1½ zig zag) for accurate control. Extra lines were worked between the stamped lines, making a continuous jagged line.

Here again, you must work to keep the stitches running sideways to avoid making heavy, blunt lines.

Fill-in:

    Side stitch is nearly always best for fill-in work. It is possible to get an accurate grainline and even stitch when working sideways.

    Fill-in stitch is not to be confused with *encroaching* stitch. The latter is made simply by placing rows of satin stitch near to or overlapping one another. This may be done by moving forward and backward, or else diagonally. This method of filling an area is good in some few instances, but is never so versatile as *side stitch fill-in*.

    To do this fill-in, set whatever zig zag you desire, then move sideways with an uneven, jogging motion, filling a small area, moving on to fill a little more, and blending the areas into one another as you go.

    A small boy was once watching me do this when he suddenly brightened and said, *Look Mommy, it's just like coloring with crayons!* And it is. You fill in with thread very much as you would color an area with crayons.

    To get the feel of this, work first with an area of straight grain, such as a block letter. For an even stitch line at the edge, place a row of stitching there first, then work away from it toward the center of the design.

    After a little practice it is no problem to rotate the hoop as you work, turning slowly and fanning the stitches out for a correct grainline on flowers, leaves, fruits or any shape you wish to make.

Line Variations:

   With machine embroidery we are free to stitch outlines in any way
we wish. For instance, a leaf intended for outline stitch may be
embroidered in a number of different ways.

   The three leaves below were stamped exactly the same. The one on
the left was simply outlined with a medium zig zag, holding the leaf
at one angle while working around it.

   The center leaf was done with wide zig zag turning as it was
worked so that a side stitch was worked on each section.

   The leaf on the right is *feather stitched*. For instruction on
this, refer to the previous page.

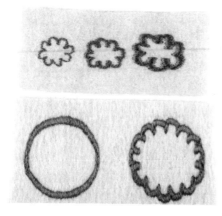

   Another variation of an outline might
be a scalloped line. A need for this sort
of line is often found at the center of a
flower. After the center itself is
embroidered, tidy up the edges next to
the petals with a scalloped line. Or maybe
just a plain circle if that is what is
called for. And remember to make the stitch
width balance with the size of the area you
are doing.

   One more interesting
shape we use frequently in
flower centers is an oval. Here are two which were
drawn exactly alike. The one on the left was done
with satin stitch while the other is side stitched.
Stitch direction *can* make a difference!

Tensions

Now, about tensions. This perhaps is the touchiest problem of all in the efficient use of a sewing machine, but it needn't be. When we understand our machines, all fear vanishes, and success is just a step away.

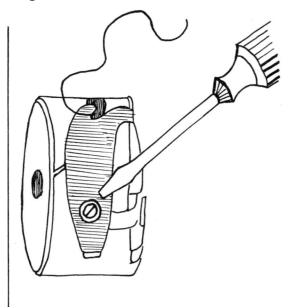

First, let's talk about a good, balanced tension for regular sewing. To get a pretty stitch and a strong seam, we must have the same amount of *pull* on both top and bottom threads. Each thread has a means of adjustment. On the bobbin case (some are removable, and some are built in) there is a small tension spring laying flat against the outside of the bobbin case. Also, there is a tiny screw which regulates the pressure of the tension spring. By tightening or loosening that little screw, we create more or less space for the thread to pull through, thus varying the tension on the bottom thread. As the thread is pulled from the bobbin case, it should feel firm and even. If it feels tight, rather than just firm, loosen the tension by turning the screw to the left, or counter clockwise. If the thread feels lax, without much firmness, tighten it by turning the little screw to the right, or clockwise. It usually takes only a fraction of a turn to make a considerable difference. If you will remember that *right* and *tight* rhyme, you can be sure you're turning the proper direction. Or, if your bobbin case has numbers, a higher number tightens, a lower number loosens.

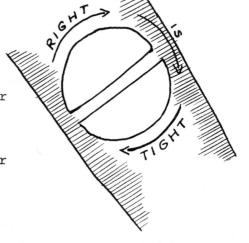

Now, with our bobbin tension adjusted correctly, we'll do all further adjusting from the top. Just remember that your thread is taking up more or less space under the tension spring; thus, you get a different tension than you may have had before.

With the top tension, as with the bottom, you'll find left will loosen and right will tighten. It's hard to say just how much to turn

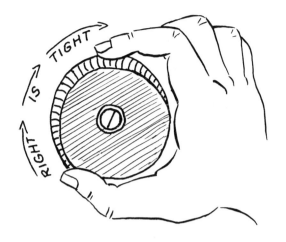

the knob—it varies so much from one machine to another. Once you experiment with your own machine and find out how to judge, you shouldn't have any more difficulty.

With the bobbin tension correct, let's learn the rules about adjusting from the top. If our stitch looks ⟋⟍⟍⟍⟍ like this, we can be sure that the *top* thread is the *looser* of the two, and that the tighter bottom thread is pulling it through to the back side of the material. We will tighten the top thread until it forces the bottom thread to meet it in the middle, like this ⟍⟍⟍⟍ . Or, if the top thread is tighter than the bottom, it will pull the bottom thread up to the top, and loops will form on the right side of the material, ⟍⟍⟍⟍ like this. To correct this, simply loosen the top tension until the threads meet in the middle to form a balanced tension. Don't be alarmed if you must turn the tension knob several times to get the results you want. Don't be discouraged. After a few tries, it will all fall into place and you'll be completely at home with adjusting tensions.

Begin to Embroider

Perhaps the best and easiest way to begin learning embroidery is to get the feel of working free of the presser foot and the feed dogs. We'll have our material in a hoop, and will need to move freely forward and back, side to side, so it's obvious that we will remove the presser foot and get rid of its interference. If we leave the feed dogs set for normal sewing, they will constantly bump up and down against the underside of our work and handicap the free movement of the hoops. On some machines, we lower the feed dogs; on others, a lever raises the plate cover above the feed dogs; on still others, a small plate snaps into place directly over them. If in doubt, consult the manual.

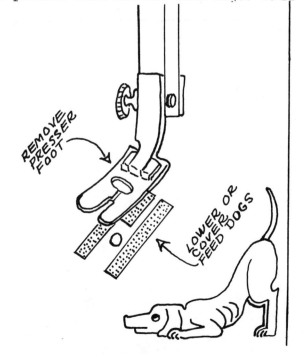

19

Now, about tension adjustment. You *will* have to adjust, to do satisfactory embroidery work. Since bobbin tension adjustment is a bit tricky, many of us find it worthwhile to buy an extra bobbin case which we can adjust for embroidery. Thus, we avoid upsetting the precision balance needed for regular sewing.

With embroidery, the *top tension must always be looser* than the bottom, but how much looser will depend on what you are doing, and the effect you want. The bottom thread must pull the top thread down and under, and away from the edges of the stitches, with only a few special exceptions. At the same time, if the top thread is *too* loose, loops of thread will form on your work, and this is not good.

For most of your work, you'll want white embroidery thread on the bobbin, and colored on the top. We may as well thread up with these while we learn the tension adjustment. (Regular thread will do, though it isn't as nice as the special thread made for machine embroidery.) The fineness of the embroidery thread will take up less space under the tension spring, giving you less *pull* on the thread. You may or may not want to adjust this—we will have to experiment to see.

If you forget to put the presser bar down, you'll know it right away, as unsightly loops will form underneath when it is left up. You must be aware from the first of remembering to put the bar down before beginning to embroider, and lift it to release the tension on the thread when you want to pull your material out.

With the presser bar down, you'll need to loosen the top tension, sometimes quite drastically. But now let's start at the beginning and do a little experimenting.

First, put a piece of practice material in the hoops. A firm, close weave is best. You need a good quality hoop, one especially made for machine embroidery.

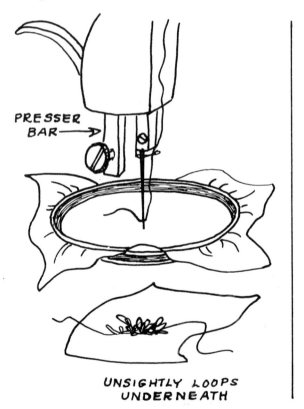

PRESSER
BAR→

UNSIGHTLY LOOPS
UNDERNEATH

Loosen the screw on the hoop a little, and lay the large ring on the table. Place material, right side up, over the hoop, and slip the

small ring inside, aligning the
lower parts of the hoop which
aids in placing the assembled
hoop under the presser bar of
most machines. Tighten the
screw, pull the material around
the edges to tighten it in the
hoop, and check the screw to
see if it can be firmed up any
more. Now, push the inside ring
through very slightly, so that
it extends about an eighth of an
inch lower than the outside ring.
This gives your material a little
extra firmness (you must have it
about as tight as a drum), and
helps prevent your hoops from
catching on the edge of the
machine bed and such places.

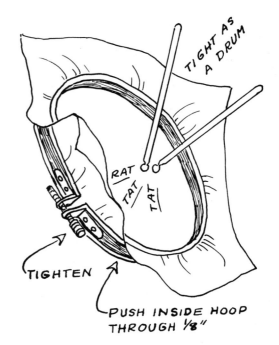

TIGHT AS A DRUM

RAT TAT TAT

TIGHTEN

PUSH INSIDE HOOP THROUGH 1/8"

Now, with feed dogs lowered
or covered, presser foot off,
embroidery thread on top and bottom, and a fairly fine needle in the
machine, you're ready to start experimenting. Draw a few lines and
designs on the material in the hoop—straight lines that are horizontal,
vertical and on an angle, a few horse-shoe shapes are good, and some
crooked snake-like lines. Keep in mind that you're not going to turn
the hoop, but will move it forward and back, side to side, any
direction you wish to go, simply sliding the hoop in that direction,
rather than turning it. It helps to pretend that the needle is a pencil,
then slide the hoop to make that pencil trace the desired line.

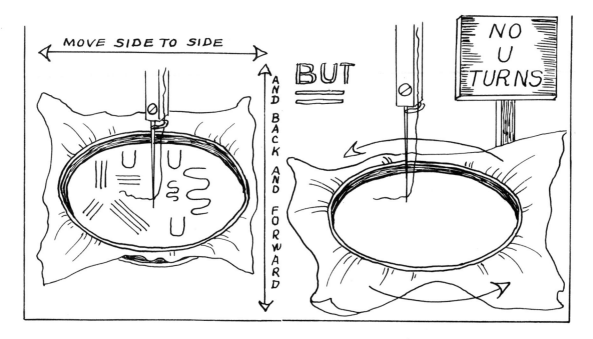

MOVE SIDE TO SIDE

AND BACK AND FORWARD

BUT

NO U TURNS

21

Let's start at the top of a vertical line and work down it, in the same direction we would go if the presser foot and feed dogs were feeding it. First bring the bottom thread up by holding the top thread and turning the balance wheel. With both threads on top, lay a finger on them for your first stitch or two, so that they won't tangle. The widest zig zag is the easiest to learn with so set your machine for that. The stitch length does not matter since we will control the length entirely with our hands. Now, start the machine slowly, letting the needle swing from side to side across the line, keeping the line about in the middle of the stitch. Keep both hands on your work with a very light pressure. If your machine doesn't start readily, give it a little more power. You should

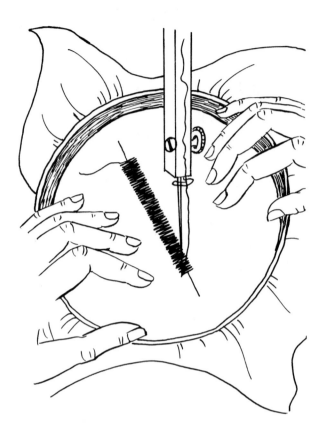

never need to start the wheel in motion with your hand. While working slowly but smoothly, try to synchronize the speed of the needle with the movement of the material, to form a nice, even line of closely packed stitches. This is called a satin stitch.

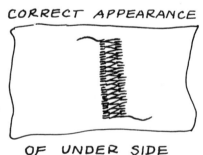

CORRECT APPEARANCE

OF UNDER SIDE

If the stitch loops are forming too near the edge of the zig zag, you need to loosen the top thread so that more comes down and under.

Now, turn your work over and inspect the wrong side. The top thread should pull down and under, meeting somewhere near the center of the zig zag stitch. In fact, almost covering the bottom thread.

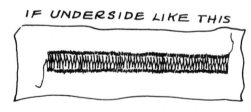

IF UNDERSIDE LIKE THIS

MUST LOOSEN TOP THREAD

If, on the other hand, the top thread is too loose, it will form unsightly loops underneath, as we mentioned before, and you must tighten the top tension.

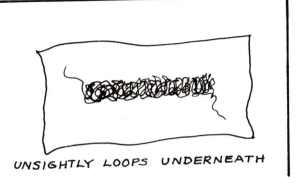

UNSIGHTLY LOOPS UNDERNEATH

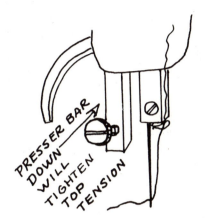

Now you must work to loosen the top tension until the top thread is loose enough to be pulled down and under by the bottom thread. When you have the proper adjustment, the thread of the top stitches will lay smooth across the top side with a look of firmness, yet not the slightest bit of pucker.

If you have been working with the presser bar up, simply putting it down will tighten the tension. In fact, it's almost sure to tighten it too much, and you will know this by the loops of bottom thread pulling up to the top.

RIGHT SIDE

UNDER SIDE

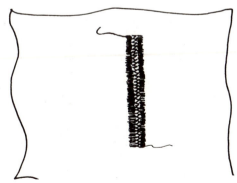

The wrong side may look all wrong until you get accustomed to it, but it's correct if the stitch loops form somewhere near the center of the zig zag, and there's a firm, but not tight, look about it. It doesn't matter if the top thread covers the bottom thread, as long as it isn't loose enough to form loops.

A little bit of experimenting with tensions at this point can be of great value to you. Just remember that you may need to turn your tension knob quite drastically to obtain the results you want. Don't be afraid to try. This may be the first step in obtaining the self-confidence you'll need to become really successful with machine embroidery.

We've worked forward on a
vertical line, or lines, and have
adjusted tensions to give the
desired effect. Now let's try
going backward up a line. You'll
soon find that you'll do a
smoother job if you can work
rapidly. After all, this is
just practice. Go ahead and
give it a whirl.

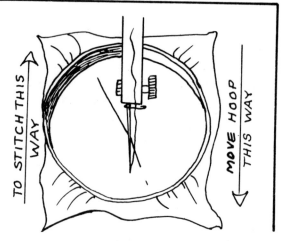

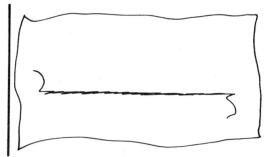

Next, try moving the hoop
sideways so the needle traces a
horizontal line. Quite a different
effect, and not very pretty, but
you'll find this sideways stitch
to be one of the most useful of
all later on.

Now, how about making a few
horseshoes? Start at the top of
one leg of the horseshoe, make a
couple of zig zag stitches and
backtrack over them so that they
are covered and there's no danger
of the thread ends pulling out.
Work forward as rapidly as you
dare, but slowly enough to keep
the stitches closely packed.
When you get to the bottom, just
go skimming across and start up
the other side rather quickly.
If you hesitate too long on the
sideways stitch, your threads
pile up in an awkward manner,
and the smooth contour is lost.
You'll learn later on how to fill
in with a sideways stitch, but for
now, let it be a thin line across
the bottom. Finish the upward side
with a close satin stitch to match
the downward side, then fasten off
the thread with a few tiny straight
stitches worked along the edge of
the satin stitch.

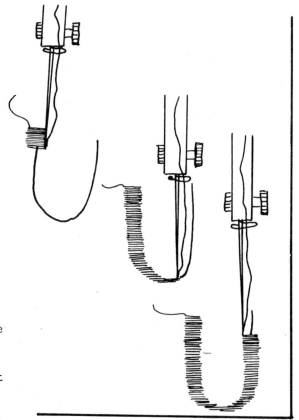

As the needle passes
in and out of the fabric,
the work must be held
firmly against the needle
plate to allow the forma-
tion of stitches. If the
material is lax, the
stitches won't form prop-
erly, if at all. So, if
you're skipping stitches,
check yourself on that
score.

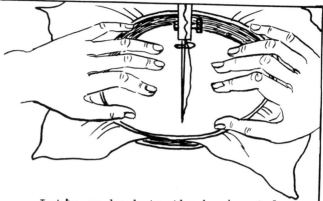

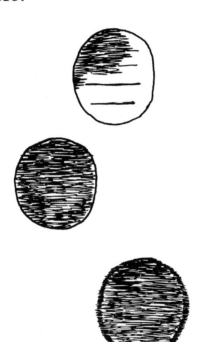

Let's go back to the horizontal
lines we touched on earlier. Draw a
small figure in your hoop—a circle will
do—with a few horizontal lines through
it. Practice moving the material gently
sideways under the needle, following
these lines. Don't try to move too
rapidly—let the zig zag do the work
for you. Now keep moving from side to
side, filling in the design as you go.
You'll soon find your own speed, and your
own best way of doing this. It usually
looks better if, rather than making one
straight row after another, you will fill
in a little patch and then move on,
constantly blending the stitches into one
another for a smooth, over-all effect.

If you wish to outline the edge, go
around it with a medium satin stitch,
sliding the hoop, but not turning it, to
follow the edge around.

You needn't break the thread here, but simply move over to the next
design. If you're using a narrow zig zag, it isn't too important to
finish off with a straight stitch, but the wider the stitch, the more
likely it is to ravel out.

You should be ready now to fill your hoop with various shapes and
designs. Your awkwardness will soon leave, and you'll find yourself
enjoying your practice. If you want to write an initial or name,
follow the lines exactly the same as you would with a pencil.

An important word here. *RELAX!!* It's easy at this point to become so engrossed in this new thing that we get our muscles all tense, and focus our eyes too intently on what we're doing. Your posture, the position of your chair, and your foot or knee on the control, will all fit in quite naturally if you will learn to pay attention to a few essentials.

Your forearms or elbows should rest on the machine bed, taking all the strain off wrists, shoulders and upper arms. Rest fingers lightly on material in the hoops. Eyes should just gaze at your work, rather than pin-point where the needle is working.

Work at first on inconsequential items, such as everyday linens and clothing. Put a design on a dishtowel and see what you can do with it. You'll have fun using that dish towel and other *first* items. Children love seeing their names on pillow cases, wash cloths, everyday shirts, etc., and your practice won't have been wasted.

One of our very good students made it a point not to go out and buy things to embroider in the beginning. Rather, she stitched designs and cute decorations on things she had on hand. In her words, *You'd be hard-put to find anything in our house that isn't embroidered.*

This led to a fine opportunity to earn a nice income from her stitching. Someone with a custom-embroidery business happened to see her lovely work on her little girl's dresses, and promptly came to ask the mother to work for him. We just never know where the opportunities might be.

Embroidering Ready-made Clothing

When shopping for clothing you wish to embroider, take a close look at the different items and see where a design might be appropriate.

On shirts and jackets, consider working on collars, cuffs, yokes, middle of the back, pockets, etc. If you wish to embroider a pocket, remove it first. Baste scrap material onto the edges to make it large enough for the hoop. A neat design along the line of the buttonholes might be interesting.

At present the fad is to load the entire shirt with embroidery, applique, etc., so anything goes.

With dresses you could place a flower or bouquet to imitate a corsage, but it's more fun to put it in an unexpected place. Think of a neat border of flowers, leaves, geometrics, paper dolls, etc., at the bottom of the skirt, on collar and sleeves. (Sleeves may need to be opened for this.) A panel of embroidery from waistline or top of dress to hemline might be good. Watch for a neckline you would like to embroider.

A design tucked into the pleat of a skirt is interesting, and a bit unexpected. A butterfly on the hip of slacks would be fun, or a caterpillar crawling on your shoulder.

If it is not convenient to use a hoop on an area, try working without one. By using a narrow stitch, putting a darning spring on the needle, and keeping your fingers on the work close to the needle, you can do small areas quite nicely.

Casual wear is especially fun for machine embroidery. You may be as flamboyant as you wish, and it looks great.

Dressy clothing calls for refinement and restraint. After doing the fun things on the casual items, you have the experience and skill for doing something elegant if you wish.

The important thing is to please your own taste, and satisfy whatever creative desires you were blessed with. Many of us love to do the spontaneous, original thing, but if this is not for you, there is an abundance of nice designs on the market from which you may choose. Follow them line-for-line if you wish, but you will likely want to use the design only as a guide and add your own innovations.

Think twice or more when deciding where to place a design. I once had a funny experience when embroidering denim jackets for our grand-daughters. Each of the four little girls chose a large design which she wanted in the middle of the back, and they watched with great anticipation as the embroidery progressed.

Upon completion, Shalane and Shannon with the short hair showed off their designs to good advantage, but Lori and Kristy had long hair which hid their embroidery. Lori slept in curlers that first night so that her hair would be held up off the embroidery for school the next day.

Consider, too, that embroidery draws attention to an area, so watch that you play up the right ones. A design too near a double chin, large bustline, thick waist, an armpit, etc., can be bad news. But a cleverly placed design can draw attention *away* from the trouble spots.

Blouse With Jersey Applique

Knits, especially those of fine, smooth texture, are especially nice for applique. A minimum amount of stitching holds them, and they are not inclined to pull away from the stitches.

Right now the jersey and knit prints are popular, so they are easy to find in the stores.

While searching for the right cotton blouse to use for showing this technique, I found this one with the interesting yoke, both front and back.

In deciding how much of the print to buy for the decoration, I tried to visualize how the different parts of the design would be arranged on the blouse, and bought accordingly. I still had to go back for six inches more to get enough small flowers.

This sort of job has to develop as you go along. First the big bird went on the back, then a flower was placed here and another there, a leaf or two added, then more flowers tucked in. Then it was draped on the back of the couch to be studied for the next addition.

In using this technique, the applique is not cut out until after the initial stitching is done. The following picture shows how the piece of jersey with the desired applique is pinned in place, and the flower outlined with sketchy stitching.

Next, the first stitching is covered with a heavier, wider stitch, and details are embroidered as desired. This is illustrated on the completed flower and leaf in the illustration.

It was a bit tricky, but a great deal of fun to put this design together. Beginning with the main part of the design (birds) then gradually adding this and that, taking time in between to ponder what should go where, it developed nicely.

One lesson I have to learn over and over is that there is a fine line between *simple* and *plain*. In this case I wanted the line of design on the front to be simple so that the birds would show off to good advantage. It seemed that a rather symmetrical line of flowers would do this, which turned out to look very plain. However, by adding a small leaf here and there, the evenness was broken up, and the combination of colors made it sing.

If you want to do something of this sort, but feel that it would be too difficult, try it anyway. An everyday shirt or jacket would be a good beginning. You may surprise yourself and find that you can be very successful. The technique adapts nicely for many kinds of work.

Pin-stripe Blouse

This seersucker blouse was a natural for embroidery. It was purchased partly because I needed a cool cotton blouse, but mainly because the stripe direction begged for some stitchery.

The first step in designing the embroidery was to sketch some stripes on paper, then doodle with a pencil until an acceptable design appeared. It had to be small and simple.

Working on the collar and yoke of the blouse, a narrow line of green satin stitch was worked along the center of each white stripe. In order to get a clean, sharp line the machine was set up for regular sewing with presser foot on and feed dogs in action.

With the straight lines completed, a ruler and pencil were used to mark a dot where the leaves and flowers were to go.

No hoop was needed here as the design was so small, and a very narrow zig zag was used. Darning spring and fingers held the material in place while the stitches were formed, and there was no puckering.

Maybe you notice sometimes, as I did while doing this blouse, that apprehensions keep creeping in as you work, and you wonder if it will turn out all right. It usually does, and a good pressing will prove it. Then when you wear it and the compliments start coming, you're sure.

It was a joy to find that the collar and neckline of this blouse actually fit even better after embroidery than before.

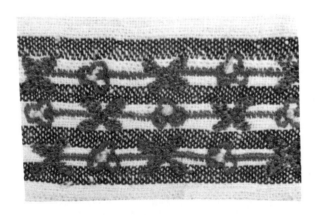

31

LURAE'S BLOUSE

Frosty white thread on a blue shirt, worked almost entirely in straight stitch makes this piece really sparkle.

The design is available and is listed in *"Sources."*

We are delighted with all of the things you can do with straight stitch embroidery, and suggest that you try it right away if you have not already done so.

For helps and ideas for this, see the chapter on *"Stitches."*

Ron's Shirt

The unique thing about this piece of embroidery is that a man did it. Very good work, too.

Ron took the Machine Embroidery class, and found that he was pretty good at it. After doing the kitty and other class projects, he decided to embroider his shirt.

Being a member of a fine quartette called *Those Guys* he had this design made for his embroidery. The other fellows were so well impressed that they acquired matching shirts, and they look pretty great in these uniforms.

Patches

Whether they be frivolous or dressy, patches can be decorative and fun. Useful, too, for covering the worn spots on clothing. The kids enjoy the comic sayings tacked onto their clothing, and they come up with some pretty clever ones.

Suggestions:
Patches for denim clothing might be made from an old piece of denim. A girl's jeans could be decorated with patches from a print from which her blouse was made. A flower or other item might be embroidered on sheer material, then appliqued onto the clothing.

You might want to make patches as the commercial ones are done, bonded to stiff material with the edges nicely finished. However, the neatest and easiest way is to do whatever embroidery is desired, then applique the patch with a satin stitched edge.

For more complete instructions on getting the patch onto the fabric turn to *Embroider Then Applique It*, page 64.

Embroider The Clothing You Make

Of course the embroidery will be done before the article is sewn together. *Do not* cut out the section to be embroidered until it is determined that the piece will be large enough to accommodate the hoop. If it is not, simply trace the pattern section onto the fabric, then cut beyond the marked area to make the piece large enough.

If the section is already cut, and is too small for the hoop, simply baste scrap material to the edge to enlarge it.

If the section is to be heavily embroidered, plan on embroidering the entire piece, as the heavy stitching may draw the fabric a little. Allow a little fabric beyond the size of the pattern piece for the same reason.

Almost every fabric can be successfully embroidered with the machine, some with greater success than others, and some which require great ingenuity. The important thing is to work with a scrap of fabric you plan to use, and change or modify your technique until you achieve success before beginning your article.

Generally, the natural fibers of medium weight and close weave respond the best, but we want to learn to adapt our work to whatever fabric we wish to use.

A few of the fabrics we have had success with are suede cloth of various types, Qiana, organza, net, raw silk, polyester chiffon, knits of all fibers, and many more. I even embroidered a pair of panty hose once. Having been the cause of my friend's panty hose being ruined, I bought her a new pair, and on the hip wrote, *Dear Gail, please forgive me.*

A few hints now on handling tricky fabrics. Of first importance is proper tension adjustment. If you need help, refer to the instructions on this, then experiment on the fabric you will be using until your stitching lays in nicely with no puckers.

There is one problem we often find in using tightly woven or tightly knit fabrics, especially the finer ones. The fabric may stick to the needle as it goes up and down, thereby causing skipped stitches and sometimes breaking the thread. This can usually be corrected by using a finer needle and putting on a darning spring. In fact, the spring is nearly always a help for any difficulty. (See *Sources*.)

Any knit, or otherwise stretchy fabric should be stretched moderately in the hoop. After embroidery when it is removed from the hoop and relaxes to its normal shape, the stitches relax with it, lessening the chance of puckering.

Using paper under the design can help prevent puckering. The reason we get puckers is that there is more *pull* on the thread than there is resistance in the material, and stiff paper underneath helps to equalize this. The paper will break away from the stitching underneath, and that which remains within the stitches matters little.

A stiff, lightweight fabric, such as organdy, may be used for backing, but should be trimmed close to the stitching so that you may press the article properly. Pellon may also be used in this way.

Some embroiderers find success in pressing lightweight iron-on facing onto the wrong side of the design area. When the embroidery is completed, the facing is peeled off with very little trimming required.

It is important that you work out these problems in your own way and find the solutions which work best for you.

Sheer Applique
(See Color Section, no pattern given)

Sheer applique is one of the easiest ways to achieve spectacular results, and the possibilities for its use are unlimited.

The applique on this dress was done for *Nannette of New York*, that adorable Bridal Boutique in Salt Lake City's Trolley Square. The dress is off-white Qiana, and is shown in full color in the center section of this book.

Here is how it was done. The design was briefly sketched on butcher paper with a clear drawing of the five different types of flowers. Having chosen the colors of nylon organdy for the applique, we used matching crayons to mark the areas of color on the paper design.

It was determined how many flowers of each color were needed, and they were traced onto the organdy, spacing them two inches apart. These were then cut into squares and stacked, ready for use.

Nannette loves the bright, glossy Mexican silk thread, and she chose colors more intense than the organdy they were to be used on. The effect is rich and beautiful. (See *Threads* chapter.)

The large flowers were done first, followed by stems and leaves. The stems were drawn on with tailor's chalk, and embroidered. Everything else in the design was appliqued.

Next, the smaller flowers were scattered, and the berries placed here and there as *fillers* wherever a little extra was needed.

To do the applique, pin a square of organdy with traced flower in place. Put the material in the hoop and if there is any worry about puckering, use paper underneath.

Whatever details are desired for the flower may be done first or last, as is convenient.

Stitch width matters not on the inside details. However, the outer edge of the design must be covered with a close, medium-to-wide satin stitch to adequately hold the applique and prevent fraying.

After the stitching is completed, before removing from the hoop, trim the organdy very close to the stitching. It helps if your scissors are not too sharp. Lift the outer edge of the organdy and pull it a little as you snip, to help cut close.

The embroidered illustration below may help you with ideas for designs.

Nannette's Jacket
(See Color Section, pattern given)

Nannette especially wanted a Lily of the Valley design for her jacket, as this is the trademark of her Bridal Boutique.

Designing the clusters of flowers was not difficult. On a large piece of paper we drew the shape of the area to be embroidered. Pictures and designs were gathered, also pencil and eraser.

First we lightly drew the general shape of the design we had in mind, and with helps from looking at the pictures we went to work.

A light hand and free motion are essential in getting a design started. Let the curves roll, and don't be afraid to try a line this way and that any number of times until it pleases you. And when you think your design is completed, leave it for a few hours or a day, then study it again. If it still *feels* right, you're ready to go ahead.

This jacket was my first experience with embroidering suede cloth and I was a bit apprehensive. Experimenting on a scrap proved that it responds beautifully, with hardly any problems.

Tips: Avoid leaving the material in the hoop longer than necessary. If hoop marks appear, rub them out with a soft cloth while pressing. Use stiff paper underneath. Steam press in the usual way, with soft fabric underneath.

My Pantsuit
(Color section, pattern given)

Suit construction by Nannette of New York, embroidery by me. If you enjoy tapered embroidery, you'll love doing wheat. If you need a brush-up on the technique, turn back to *Stitches*.

This embroidery design is made to be used singly, or as a repeat by turning the pattern over on alternating patterns. I can think of nothing lovelier than a border of this wheat across the hem of a sheet, or down the center of a tablecloth.

The suit is of suedecloth, and of course was embroidered before the seams were sewn. Beyond the usual precautions (careful tension adjustment, paper under) there were no problems in working with the fabric.

To avoid excessive hoop marks, remove the fabric as soon as possible. Steam press right away, rubbing out any marks with a cloth or soft brush.

I'm so glad that Nannette likes my embroidery work for her shop. Her taste and ideas are clever and unusual, her fabrics are gorgeous and a challenge to embroider, and it's exciting to help work out her plans. She does exquisite dressmaking, and we often trade work, just for fun.

Embroider a Knit
by Linda Zachary Goff

We all wear and sew on polyester fabrics much of the time today. Knits of all kinds are really *today's fabrics* so we must know how to embroider them with ease.

Special Techniques:

There are three things we must do for all knits: 1) Use a ball point needle, size 70 or 11. 2) Use a darning spring at all times to help control the stretch while the needle goes in and out of the material taking the stitches. 3) Stabilize the stretch temporarily while doing the embroidery. We will discuss each kind of knit with suggestions for that particular knit.

Kinds of Knits:

Polyester double knit—These heavier knits are so easy to embroider if we are careful. Carefully put the material in the hoops so the crosswise and lengthwise stretches are evenly firm. If either or both are stretched onto the bias, puckering and rippling will result when the fabric is taken out of the hoops. A heavy paper like type or notebook paper can then be placed under the hoops.

A second way to stabilize these knits, and my favorite, is to use a bondable interfacing on the back side of the fabric just under the design to be embroidered. I find that by bonding this interfacing to the backside before placing it in the hoops, all chance of stretching in the hoops is eliminated. After the embroidery is completed, the inter-facing serves no function and can be cut away or left in place. Be sure to use a light or feather weight interfacing as its function is to stabilize the stretch, not to stiffen.

Single knits—Nylon tricot, Qiana, blouse weight knit, cotton-polyester blend. These knits are usually lightweight and worn loosely over the body so again we do not want to stretch these knits in the hoops. Simply lay type paper under the knit and put both the knit and paper into the hoops. By putting the paper into the hoop with the fabric, any chance of stretching in the hoops is reduced. These knits are too thin or sheer to use the interfacing as the outline of it would show through to the top side and be unattractive.

Super stretchy knits—Rib knit, swimwear, leotard fabric, lingerie fabrics. Lay a piece of heavy paper under the hoops while sewing these knits. These knits usually have to be stretched in the hoops because they are worn over the body in a stretched position.

Calculate the amount of stretch by measuring one inch with the garment off the body. Then put the garment on the body and measure how far the inch is stretched. Put the garment into the hoops and stretch the inch to the correct amount.

Caution:

We must limit most of our work on knits to only outlining. However, when fill-in is needed, let us suggest using a sketchy fill-in. By limiting the number of stitches, we also limit fabric damage and puckering or buckling.

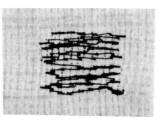

If a very solid fill-in is a must, consider appliqueing the design after it is filled in solid on another piece of cloth. Very light weight material is best to use under these designs to be appliqued to knits. Be careful to preshrink both fabrics as the shrinking of either one will result in puckering.

Embroider Vinyl and Leather

(See Color Section, pattern given)

This vest is made of heavy vinyl with firm backing, one of the easiest to use for embroidery. Read the instruction given here, then experiment with various types of vinyl for making clothing, bags, pillows, etc.

Here are some of the things we learned while embroidering this design: #50 thread broke frequently, and caused buckling of the design. Changing to #30 corrected both problems, and the design laid nice and smooth.

Use fine needles on vinyl. However, needles are dulled more readily than in sewing on fabric, and a dull needle contributes to thread breakage.

Lay paper under your work to help it glide freely over the needle plate.

For transferring a design onto vinyl, the art tracing method is preferred (see *Transferring the Design*) since a hot iron cannot be used on this material.

Tip:
Instead of sewing hems, glue them. Use a strong, fast drying cement.

Leather:
Barbara Brower with the help of her son, Karl, has been designing and working on tanned deer hide to make a jacket for Karl. Through much trial and error she learned some valuable things, and is glad to share them for the benefit of all of us.

Regular needles will not work, but a chisel point leather needle does a fine job. Ask your sewing machine dealer to get it for you. Stiff paper or iron-on facing is a must to keep the leather from stretching. A spring or preferably a darning foot is essential. Size 30 thread is best, as it takes less stitches to cover the fabric. This is important, as each stitch cuts a hole in the leather, and the less stitches, the better.

There is still much research to be done before leather embroidery can be really successful with home style machines. We will continue to experiment and learn and have more for you in the future. If you have any truths you would like to share with us, please do.

Combine Paint and Stitching
(Color section, pattern packet)

Nothing could be easier or more fun than coloring the large areas of a design, then embroidering the outline and details.

Fabric paints of different kinds are popular and easy to come by, and are simple to apply. For this project *Fabric Crayons* by Crayola were used. The instructions on the box are simple to follow, and it is important that you do exactly as it says.

Let me tell you how the Ballerinas were done. Pale pink fabric was chosen, making pink little girls. The rayon content accepts the crayons nicely.

Hot iron transfer patterns from the pattern packet were prepared by coloring the desired areas with the crayons. The coloring was then brushed to remove any specks, and this is important. Even though the specks are not visible, they show up later as blotches.

Prepare the ironing board, fabric and patterns as directed on the box. As you press with hot iron, the design and color are transferred, and you are ready to embroider. The transferred colors may be different than what you would expect so it is wise to test them on a scrap first.

Embroidering was done in the very most simple way—outline for the most part, with narrow side-stitch for the skirt gathers.

After these were mounted and framed, they seemed to lack a little something, so I used one of my favorite tricks — narrow velvet ribbon glued just inside the frame.

Versatile Rose
(Color section, pattern packet)

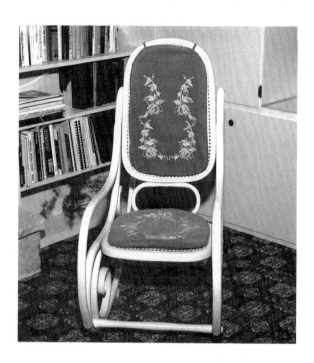

This lovely design was made specifically to be used as a repeat pattern, and is nice by itself also. Form it into a circle as on the seat, or into a graceful border by reversing the design, as on the back. Wouldn't a row of these gently curving across the hem of a sheet be delightful? Or maybe down the front of a pretty robe?

The fabric for the cushions is suede cloth. Simple outline stitch was used for most of the work. For accenting the leaves and part of the petals, a straight stitch *filler* was used. To differentiate, the leaves got straight lines, the flower petals a *squiggle* effect. This is shown in the stitched illustrations below.

The smallest leaves are *tapered* lazy daisy, but would be nice if done in outline or fill-in. The tiny circles placed here and there are simple outline. These small details make a lot of difference.

In constructing the cushions, a little padding was needed, which called for quilting. We didn't want to risk spoiling the roses with added stitching, and since the fabric was firm enough to stand alone, we did something a bit unusual. The lining material and batting were quilted together, then the cushions were made.

Adapt or Create

Perhaps you enjoy copying a design line-for-line, and if this gives you satisfaction you should pursue it.

For many of us, using established designs and adapting them for specific needs is desirable. For others, the only way to go is to design it from the beginning. For all of us, our needs and desires will change as we improve our skills. Perhaps you find, as I do, that the happiest times are when the creative juices are running.

Adapt a Design:
This subject covers a wide range, but let's pinpoint a couple of things for the sake of a beginning.

Problem: You need a small design to embroider on a pointed collar. One design which you like is the right size, but is round and would not fit the shape of the collar.

Solution: (Example given in the drawings below.) Trace the collar onto transparent paper. Sketch on this the general shape you want for the design. Lay this over the round design and see how you might make the changes that would make it fit. Turn the design this way and that, trace a leaf here, a flower there, curve a stem to fit, turning and tracing and making changes until it pleases you.

Try to determine why you like the design and work to maintain that quality as you make the changes. If it is the gracefully curving lines, work to keep those lines flowing. Or maybe the design is symmetrical and that pleases you. Do all you can to keep it that way as you make the necessary changes.

Wheat Tablecloth

Speaking of adapting designs, would you believe that the wheat on this cloth was designed to be flowers?

This tablecloth is one I did in 1964 for my parents' Golden Wedding Anniversary. My goal was to embroider the perfect cloth for their round table, with wheat to match their dishes.

The department stores had many linen cloths stamped for embroidery, but none with wheat. And then I saw it...a design with sprays of tiny flowers which might be adapted! While studying this, I said aloud to myself, *I think I can make wheat of that.* A saleslady nearby quickly assured me that indeed I could not, and that's when my Merrell determination came forward. (My husband chooses to call it stubbornness.)

With my treasure I hurried home to the machine, and soon had the project underway. And what a joyful project it was!

The pattern is not given in the book, because it was a commercial design, but I'll show you what the original was like and how the changes were made.

Create a Design
(In full color, center section)

This creation which I call *Hills of Home* reveals the influence of my Southwest heritage. Let me tell you how this picture developed, and it may give you an idea for doing something close to your own heart.

My artist friend, Colleen Parker, gave me guidance. Having chosen the frame and the wall space, and knowing that I wanted something reminiscent of the desert, I invited Colleen over to help me plan it.

It was interesting to see her at work. Sitting across the room from where the picture would hang, she studied the details of furnishings, colors, etc., then turned to the materials I had gathered to consider using.

From several different background fabrics, she chose natural linen of rather a dark tone, because it picked up the color of the fireplace stone.

My file of Southwest pictures was saved from magazines, paper napkins, newspaper ads, department store sacks, etc., and from among these we chose a yucca.

I wanted texture to play an important part in this work, and planned to use various fabrics to obtain this texture. Colleen caught the feeling of what I wanted to do and sketched in the hills and the yucca, then left me to work it out.

For the landscape I went to my collection of scraps lovingly
called *junque*; these bits of fabric were gathered from relatives,
clothing manufacturers, upholstery workshops, fabric salesmen's
kits, garage sales, you name it. My husband says "Other people have
collections. You have accumulations."

In order to tie in with the colors in the room, I needed greens
with yellowish tone, and browns in the coppery range. It must all
be very earthy and warm appearing.

Nylon organdy in a brown shade was perfect for distant hills. A
piece of sweater material was the right color and texture for the main
background fabric, and the other fabrics are various upholstery velours
and velvet. The small cacti, too, are velour. A scrap of beige-brown
sweater knit is the basis for the yucca trunks.

Funny thing—my Dearly Beloved didn't think much of this picture
while it was in the making. Thought it was just a bunch of scraps
thrown together. After living with it awhile, he loves the warmth and
simplicity of it, and would like me to pursue this technique.

48

Method:

In this picture it is obvious that the background must go on first. The distant hills were sketched onto the linen, then a rectangle of organdy was laid over this, and the sketched line was sewn with a fine satin stitch. The surplus organdy was trimmed close to the stitching above the hills, and the lower edge of organdy was simply covered by the next layer of fabric.

The large piece of sweater material came next, and was stitched rather unevenly at the top, suggesting a bit of roughness in the terrain.

Sketchy lines of stitching make the rather vague little hills in the vicinity of the yucca.

Other fabrics were layered to make the foreground, placing them this way and that until it felt good, then trimming them and stitching in place.

To get the effect of the sandy bank in the foreground, a soft, almost drapable upholstery velour was used. The thread is #30 for a coarse effect, and is somewhat darker than the fabric. The stitches run vertically on the edge of the bank, extending downward to cut into the face of it, as if there had been a hard rain. And it's a good thing you can see the picture or you'd never know what I'm talking about.

In doing a work such as this, don't be in a hurry to get it done. It needs time and thought, and a lot of warm feeling if it is going to develop in a natural way.

The foreground could use more detail, but I felt that the small cactus gave balance to the area, and I wanted it simple. After all, I spent my growing-up years tramping through terrain that looked just like this, and believe me, it's plain!

To do the Yucca:

The picture showing the detail is large (3/4 actual size) and almost needs a page by itself. The tricks involved in doing these are not difficult, and reading about it may help you sometime on a project of your own.

The trunks were cut from heavy grey-brown sweater material, and pinned in location. In real life, these trunks are quite shaggy, and light in color. Beige thread of heavy weight worked sketchily with a jagged motion produced the desired effect.

The poles were done next, so that they would appear to be growing from the center of the head. We used to call them *oose* poles, and I've wondered where the word came from. Maybe Indian?

For a lengthy appearance, the stitches run lengthwise, with small outward jags of stitching at frequent, but uneven intervals. The thread color on these is darker than the real thing, but was chosen for color balance.

A million little swords make up the body of the yucca, and these can be tricky to embroider. Let's see what we can do to simplify it.

To get started, a number of straight lines are drawn with a pencil from the center of the body outward in all directions.

Two shades of green help to get depth into this. Using the darkest shade, a straight stitch traces all of these lines. To keep it from getting bunchy in the middle, the lines are stitched from tip to tip, rather than going out and back on each spear.

After about half enough spears are done, change to the lighter green and continue until the results are satisfactory. If it looks like no other specimen in the world, maybe we have just invented a new strain.

The flowers appear difficult, and they would be if we tried to do individual blossoms. Embroidering just the form of a cluster such as this is simple, and gives the desired effect.

This is the way we do it. Since the real flowers are creamy white velvet, we wanted to use silk thread for them. We had pale yellow, and white. Combined, they made the right color. Using yellow first, we covered the form of the cluster with sketchy serpentine stitch of narrow zig zag. (See *Stitches*) Next, we threaded up with white and went over it again with the same serpentine, until the right effect was attained.

Notice that the pole extends up through the flower head. In reality, each flower is on a short stem which grows from the pole. As kids, we used to gather our aprons full of these lovely egg-sized cups, and float them down the ditch, pretending that they were sea-going ships.

After the picture was finished, mounted, framed and hung, it occurred to me that the sky seemed somehow vacant. So I cheated. I did—I glued those birds in the sky. Just little strands of black string, applied with white glue, and you would need a magnifying glass to see that they **were** not stitched. They make a nice difference in the over-all appearance of the picture, and I'm counting on you not to tell.

Quilting

General Instructions:

Quilting may be used for many things, and the speed of doing it on the machine makes it versatile indeed.

The bonded batting which has come into popular use is certainly a help. It holds together so that you can handle it almost like a fabric. This batting comes in a variety of thicknesses, and can be easily split for added or lessened thickness, depending on the puffiness desired in the quilted item.

Traditionally, quilting requires a fabric top and lining, with soft padding in between. This is still true for a cover, wrap, or other item where both sides will be seen.

However, when quilting a pillow top, wall hanging, picture to be framed, or other item which will have the back side covered, only the top and bonded batt are needed.

In making a quilt or coverlet, it is possible and practical to sew the top, lining, and batt together wrong side out, then turn it with the edges all finished before the quilting is started. Complete instructions for doing this are found in *Creative Machine Embroidery*, Volume 2, page 151.

For machine quilting it is practical to pin the fabric and batting together with large safety pins, removing them as you sew.

The quilting may be done with the presser foot and feed dogs in action on straight or gently curving lines. Care must be taken to keep both upper and lower fabrics smooth to avoid sewing puckers into your work. Help the material gently through the machine with your hands, but avoid pulling it lest you break a needle.

For free quilting, replace the presser foot with a spring for very light weight quilting or a darning foot when using a thick batt. With the spring or darning foot hopping up and down, the quilt may be moved freely under the needle as we do for embroidery.

There is a wide choice of threads for quilting. For long quilting lines, the strength of regular sewing thread or nylon invisible thread is needed. For freely embroidering a design while quilting, embroidery thread will be strong enough if zig zag is used. For straight stitch a stronger thread is preferred.

In choosing thread color, use a sharp contrast for a bright, cheerful effect. If a subdued effect is preferred, matching colors are better. For a minimum of thread showing, use *nylon invisible* either top, bobbin, or both.

Holly Hobbie Pillows

A delightful print such as this may be found now and then by keeping an eagle eye on the fabric departments. Buy ahead when you find something you really like and have it on hand to make up for a spur-of-the-moment gift. (See *Sources*.) Better still, make a few in advance.

In order to help you in doing such an item, let us point out a few basic helps.

Bonded batting of medium thickness is desirable for puffiness. Cut it larger than the design and trim after the quilting is done and the ruffle sewn in place.

Simplicity of design is important, followed by simplicity of stitching. Don't be tempted to over-embroider as too much stitching flattens the design.

As a general rule use a #2 zig zag for bold lines. Fine details will be prettier if a narrow stitch is used, #1 or less. On this design even a straight stitch might be used on the face, hands, hair, flowers, and grass. Stitch just the outline of the face. Doing the facial features on this small area would tend to distort it. Embroider only a few lines of hair close to the face and around the edges, and let the rest be full and puffy.

Such an item as this is good for a beginning, and can also be a joy forever.

A Hasty Quilt

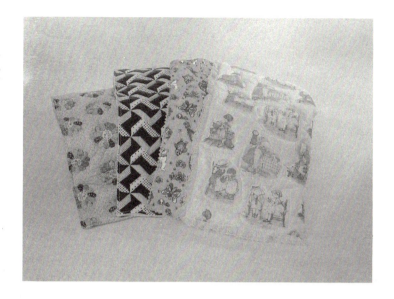

These are small quilts, very quick to make and loved by kids of all ages for TV watching, etc.

Find a print you like and soft fleece for lining. A thick bonded batt is nice for these.

Choose strong thread in matching or contrasting color. Consider using #10 nylon invisible thread (See *Sources*). These threads may be used separately or together. The nylon thread is almost invisible and gives a hand quilted look rather than machine stitched appearance.

If you wish to quilt around each design, use a spring or embroidery foot with feed dogs out of action. If the batt is thick, the foot does the better job. Simply zip around the desired area with a straight stitch.

If you want to quilt long straight lines common to hand quilting, put the presser foot on, activate the feed dogs, set a straight stitch with medium to long stitch length and let the machine feed the quilt through. You get nice even stitches this way, but you must take care and lift the weight of the quilt ahead of the needle so that it can feed properly.

If the bulk of the quilt makes it difficult to manage, simply roll one edge to the center the full length of the quilt and pin the roll with large safety pins. This will slip nicely through the head of the machine, letting you do a whole row of stitching before having to adjust the roll.

Giraffe Wall Hanging

Technique Instruction:

Quilting—Giraffe Wall Hanging. This print had been in the drawer for a long time, and suddenly the time was right for using it. Our newly decorated guest room called for the color and whimsical design of this piece.

Since this was to be a lined hanging, I had the option of quilting the lining with the stitching, or just quilting the print with the bonded batt, then putting the lining on after. I chose the latter because the urge to do this work came at a time when all the stores were closed, and I had no lining. Besides, I really think that these hang better when lined after the quilting.

Materials:
1. Giraffe panel print.
2. Bonded batt cut to the size of the panel. The thickness of the batt determines the puffiness of the quilting. Bonded batts are made in layers, enabling you to split layers for desired thickness.
3. A few large safety pins for pinning it together.

4. Machine embroidery thread of a sharp, dark color to accent the design. My choice is usually D.M.C. color 3371, a dark black-brown.
5. Suitable lining material and binding. A favorite binding for this sort of thing is polyester woven double-fold. Take the article with you when shopping for trim.

Method:

If any details on the animal are to be embroidered, this should be done before the padding is applied. Otherwise you might have bulges in rather strange places on the creature. The giraffes were to be simply outlined, with no details, so all of the stitching is done through both the fabric and padding.

Lay the panel on the batting, and pin every few inches with safety pins.

Set up the machine by removing the presser foot and replacing it with an embroidery foot or a darning spring. Put feed dogs out of action. Thread up with chosen thread, both top and bottom. Set medium zig zag and test the stitching on a scrap. Tensions should be fairly firm in order to achieve a puffiness in the quilting.

It is usually best to begin quilting in the center of an article and work out toward the edges. In planning this panel, I decided to simply outline the giraffes with no detail, since they were silhouettes.

After the animals were done, the border of leaves was next. These were to frame the animals, and should be simple. Too much stitching would flatten the area, but too little would look skimpy. So I began by doing just the main leaves and flowers all around, then after studying it, adding stitching here and there until it appeared balanced and *felt* right.

After the stitching I took it to the store to shop for the rod and the binding. It's worth a lot to let the people in the stores know you and the sort of work you do, so that they may be of help to you. I truly appreciate the salespeople here in our town of Bountiful who help me in so many ways with these things.

Keep your bindings and trimmings simple. Some of us are inclined to look for a pretty trim to show off our work, but it will usually only detract from it. For instance, a jumbo rick rack might have looked quite well on this picture, but it surely would draw the eye to the trim and away from the subject.

Quilted Rose

This is one of those lovely panel prints we run across now and then. It is done in the very most simple way, which is often the best way.

Let me point out again that quilting should be done only on outlines and separation lines, except in special instances. Any embroidery of detail usually goes on before the padding is added. Detail stitching worked through the padding will flatten or distort the design and is usually not desirable.

This piece was to be mounted on plywood, so a fabric backing was not necessary. The print was pressed, then fastened to thin bonded batting with safety pins.

No hoop is needed for this type of work, but a darning spring or an embroidery foot is a must. Oh, it's possible to work without one of these devices, but your hands get mighty tired and your arms fall off.

Narrow satin stitch outline is the main stitch used for quilting. Finest details get finest stitches, bold areas need heavier stitching.

For most outline and accenting a dark, sharp thread color is desirable, but on this one the light, bright greens seemed best for stems, calyx, and leaves.

When the stitching was completed the item was temporarily fastened to the plywood backing with thumbtacks. The quilted item should be simply laid in place with no stretching, and tacked every few inches at the edge of the wood.

Now stand it on edge the way it will hang and leave it in an upright position for a day or two. This should determine if there will be any *sag* in the quilted piece. If there is, adjust it by re-positioning a few tacks. Once it is hanging correctly, fasten at close intervals with a stapler, keeping as near the edge as possible. Then trim the fabric even with the board, and secure into the frame.

Many have said that this is one of the most attractive things I have done, and it was surely one of the quickest and easiest.

Window Valance   page 118

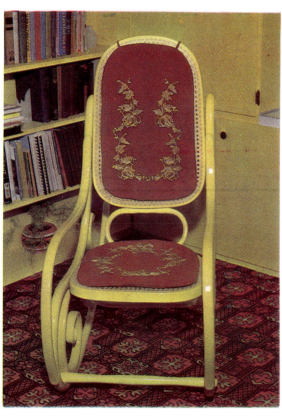

Versatile Rose   page 44

Quilted Rose   page 58

Shelly's Apron   page 90

Midnight Sparkle   page 98

Fantasyland Castle   page 93

Sheer Applique   page 36

Footstool   page 67

Crewel Embroidery   page 71

Crimson Glory   page 61

Harvest Time   page 60

Hills of Home   page 47

Album Cover Designs   page 70

Ron's Shirt   page 32

LuRae's Blouse   page 32

Vinyl Jacket   page 42

Mother's Christmas Present   page 96

Nannette's Jacket   page 38

My Pant Suit   page 39

Perky Peacock   page 91

Combine paint and stitching   page 43

Mats for Your Treasured Photos   page 101

Embroider a Printed Fabric

Prints come and go, and if you see one you like, you'd better buy it lest it be all gone when you go back later.

I never consider it an extravagance to buy a piece of fabric to be embroidered *someday*. While waiting for that day to come, it's fun to treasure the lovely items in the drawer and anticipate working them up.

Panel Prints:
There are several types of panel prints, and many interesting ways of using them in embroidery work. Here are a few of the places you might look for them:

1. Dress panels—Many exquisite designs which are suitable for wall hangings or framed pictures.
2. Drapery panels—Often very large, very beautiful designs for working up into a room divider, or large hanging.
3. Animal prints—Usually made of washable cotton, these are suitable for pillows or sleeping bags for the youngsters, also for hangings and pictures. Some are in natural settings with jungle foilage, etc., others are adorable cartoon-type designs.
4. Linen dishtowels—These have all kinds of designs, and vary from year to year. This Bicentennial Year there are many towels of a souvenier theme. Other years we have found elegant florals, birds, outdoor scenes, etc.
5. Miscellaneous sources might be dress yardage, terry towels, sheets, in fact anything made of fabric could be a source of things you might like to embroider.

Suggested Techniques:
You may wish to simply quilt a panel for a hanging, as the giraffe is done, a framed picture as the rose, or a pillow such as the Holly Hobbie.

Perhaps your need is to accent the print on a section of an item of wearing apparel, as in Volume 2, page 86.

Embroidered with solid fill-in, a printed fabric makes a lovely picture or sofa pillow. (See *Harvest Time.*)

Embroidered solid, then cut out and appliqued, you gain a depth and dimension impossible to attain any other way. (See *Crimson Glory.*)

Harvest Time

From an ordinary linen tea towel to a beautiful work of art—this is the kind of transformation you can make in a few hours of joyful stitching

An interesting thing keeps showing up in my embroidery work, and you will perhaps notice the same thing in your own work. *Always,* I do more embroidery than first intended.

In doing this piece I started at the lower right hand corner and filled in or shaded each item in quite a nice way. After moving the hoop and filling another area, I discovered that my work was getting heavier and richer along the way. It was no problem, however, to go back and work over the previous embroidery to make it equally heavy.

The corn is done with the equivalent of French knots, though some of them are so large that it was necessary to move from side to side in order to fill in the area. In outlining each kernel with dark brown (DMC 3371), the kernels stand out individually and take on a nicely rounded appearance.

The technique used in embroidering the apple is described in the Stitch Glossary under *Straight Stitch for Contours*.

There are three clusters of berries in the picture. You will see that the stitch direction varies on the different berries within each cluster. This gives them the appearance of lying at different angles and avoids a stiffness.

In studying the finished picture, I can see that every technique used is described and illustrated in the Stitch Glossary. Perhaps this will be of help to you in some way.

Crimson Glory
(Shown in color section)

This picture started out as a linen kitchen towel. The gorgeous roses were printed on an ugly grey background which, of course, I had no intention of using.

The original idea was to do a quilted effect, using a backing of thin bonded batting. I would just stitch through the two layers, outlining the petals, leaves, etc., then cut out the whole design and applique it onto a suitable background.

As usual I got carried away with embroidery and ultimately had the entire design heavily filled, shaded and accented. The batting backing helped achieve greater depth of stitching and the resulting thickness made a nicely raised applique.

By this time I had acquired the frame I wanted to use, and it was of different proportions than the rose design. So I cut the arrangement into sections and with Gail's help rearranged it.

Taking this a step at a time, let's see how each part of the process developed.

Materials used:
    Linen towel with rose design.
    Thin bonded batting the size of the towel (optional).
    Mexican silk thread in shades of red and green, some variegated.
    Suede cloth of creamy beige, four inches larger than the frame.
    Picture frame.

Method:
    Choose your threads. Other threads would have been nice for these roses, but the *silk* thread from Mexico is so lustrous and beautiful. If you are lucky you might find this thread under the *Iris* label, or other. (See *Threads.*)

    If you plan to use a backing of batting, secure it to the fabric with safety pins and avoid possible pin pricks.

Place material in hoop. Decide where you want to start and thread the machine accordingly. If you are an artist, you will have little trouble knowing where to place the different shades of thread. For most of us, though, we can rely on the printed design to guide us. These roses were beautifully shaded in the printing, so there was little question where to put the darks and the lights. Also, the grainline of the petals and leaves was clear in the design, and that was a great help with stitch direction.

Speaking of stitch direction, let's point out how this can work for us in doing these rose petals.

In working the length of a petal, the zig zag running lengthwise forms the correct grainline. As long as the needle swings in the direction you want the grainline to go, it will be correct. Fan the stitches out a little by turning the material slightly as you work. The picture below shows this quite clearly.

Where an abrupt contrast of direction is needed, as on the petal tips where they curl back, you might run the stitches in the opposite direction to achieve this. Changing from a wide to narrow zig zag helps, too. However, the narrow stitch produces a finer effect, and you may need to pile stitches upon stitches for the correct thickness.

The amount of embroidery you put on this sort of thing will be governed by your own inclinations. This rose picture would have been lovely using the original idea, but I would have missed a lot of fun.

After all of the embroidery is completed, get ready for the applique. There are two different ways of doing this:

1. Cut out the embroidered item, pin in place and applique by first stitching sketchily around it, then going around again with stitching to match the depth and direction of the embroidery.

2. Before cutting out the item, pin the whole piece in place. Stitch sketchily around the edge of the embroidery. Now cut away the surplus close to the stitching. Go over the cut edge, this time stitching to match the depth and direction of the embroidery.

In doing this kind of work it is possible to add to, take away, or change at will. In doing this particular piece it worked well to put the flowers in place, lining up stems in a logical manner, then placing the leaves and buds for balance.

The three upper flowers seemed to fall in place, and then I was stalled in deciding what to do with the lower two. That's when I sought Gail's help, and she soon had it on the way to completion.

Here again, the suede cloth proved to be very easy to work with. In pressing the completed item I used extra thicknesses of soft material (two folded dishtowels instead of one), and pressed in the usual way. Hoop marks on the fabric were rubbed out with a soft cloth.

The frame is one we found in Mexico, and matches our bedroom furniture. My husband is happy to have at last the embroidered roses he has longed for.

Embroider, Then Applique It

This technique covers a broad spectrum, and you will find that using it just once will open doors for using it many different ways. One great advantage in using this method—you know how your finished embroidery will look before it goes on the article.

A few suggestions:

A print on a fabric might suggest that you use it as an applique. Put the print in the hoop and embroider it, then applique it.

A small terry towel with mushroom or other delightful design might adapt well for a toss pillow. Embroider whatever details you wish, then applique it.

An article of wearing apparel needs some heavy embroidery. In putting heavy embroidery on soft fabric, there's a great risk of puckering. If the embroidery is done first on another piece of fabric and appliqued afterward, the risk is minimal. Even if you should make some puckers while embroidering the applique, it seldom harms the finished product.

Applique Technique:

Do not cut out the embroidered applique at this time, and do not put the material in the hoop for this next step. You will need to use a darning foot or spring, however.

Pin the embroidered piece in place, and with darning foot or spring stitch sketchily around the edge of the embroidered design. A straight stitch or very narrow zig zag may be used. The reason for no hoop for this step is that the risk of puckering is much less without it for this particular thing.

Now with small scissors trim the excess fabric away and prepare for the final stitching.

Put the design in the hoop and finish the edges by duplicating stitch direction and technique of the embroidery, thus securing the applique and covering the cut edge.

If you wish, you may stitch around the main parts of the applique to further secure it to the fabric. Perhaps leaving some of the detail embroidery to be done at this point would also help.

Sunflower Sofa Pillow

This is the easiest kind of embroidery there is. The design is there for you, colors are indicated on the print, and the design usually shows which way to go with the stitches.

Since this pillow is an item for casual use, a bold gay appearance was desirable, calling for a fun-loving approach to the work. No rich, heavy embroidery this time.

The sunflower was a scrap of printed sailcloth saved from a house-coat I made years ago. (You might get the idea that I'm a nut for sunflowers, and it's true.)

Being a firmly woven fabric, this embroidery was especially easy to do. However, almost any fabric can be embroidered if you use the correct tension adjustment and appropriate threads and needles.

Materials:
In embroidering this sunflower, a coarse appearance was desirable, so #30 thread was chosen. Three colors suffice—light orange to blend with the flower, light brown to accent the petals and make the background for the center, and very dark brown for the *seeds*. Gold no-wale corduroy is the pillow material, and brown ball fringe.

Method:
Place the printed fabric in the hoop. Using the orange thread and wide zig zag, run streaks of stitching lengthwise on all of the petals from the base outward toward the end of the petals. Work at random, or as indicated by the design.

Next, thread up with the light brown and work random streaks, this time going no more than half way out the petals, and working a little more heavily near the center.

Work the center in the light brown, using narrow zig zag and
sideways motion for a flat appearance. Cover the entire center in
this way.

The *seeds* are a series of dark brown *bumps*. To make these,
set a wide zig zag and work as you would for French knots. Hold the
fabric in one position while stacking up stitches for the desired
size. Move just a little and make another one, then another and
another, moving at random, making the bumps uneven for a natural look.

With narrow zig zag, outline the center with small scallops.
If you have a question on this, see *Stitches, Line Variations*.

The embroidery is now finished, but don't cut it out yet. Give
the piece a good pressing, then pin in place on the pillow top.

Do *not* put it in the hoop at this point. We have found that using
a hoop at this stage causes puckering. Instead, just lay the work
under the needle, and with the embroidery spring stitch sketchily around
the entire design.

Cut away the surplus fabric, and then put the item in the hoop.
Embroider over the cut edges, taking care to use the same stitch
direction as used on the first embroidery. Besides doing the cut edges,
make random streaks of color down into the petals. Also stitch separation lines wherever one petal joins another. This not only adds color
interest, but helps to secure the applique.

When the embroidery is finished, press it again and you are ready
to put the pillow together.

Sunflower Footstool
(Shown in color center section)

Perhaps you will never make a footstool, but I'll bet you will use this method of embroidery in a lot of ways. It's one of the easiest ways in the world to obtain spectacular results in a short while.

The adorable little stool was made by my brother, Leroy—the one who is so good at woodwork.

Suedecloth is the background fabric, chosen because it is durable, easy to manipulate for upholstering, and just the right color for my hearth.

To prepare for embroidering, the sunflower (pattern included in packet) was traced onto a sheer white fabric—polyester chiffon in this case because I had a scrap on hand. This was placed in a hoop large enough to accommodate the entire design with a sheet of paper underneath. The paper stabilizes the stitching on the soft fabric and shows up the traced lines of the design for ease in embroidering.

Threads chosen were #30 for fast fill-in and heavy build-up. Colors are bright sunflower yellow, medium orange, and rust, with a bit of brown-black to accent the center.

Each petal was embroidered first with the yellow thread, using a rather slow sideways motion for heavy build-up. Beginning at the base of the petal and working outward, the stitches were fanned out toward the petal tips. Since I wanted the flowers to be heavily embroidered, I built the stitching deeper on the outer portions of the petals, thus compensating for the extra stitching which would come later with the darker colors toward the center.

With the yellow completed, orange was added, stitching from the base of each petal toward the tip, and working at random in long and short streaks for a natural appearance.

Rust goes on next. With straight stitch, a separation line is made where each petal joins another. For the streaks, a medium wide zig zag is used. These streaks are shorter and fewer than those of orange. Be a little dramatic with these streaks if you wish. The base of each petal is covered completely with rust.

Without changing the thread, the flower center is covered with tiny circular stitching, using narrow zig zag. *See Filler Stitches.*

Black and yellow are used for details of the center with scalloped circles of graduated sizes and French knots added as desired. (In case you're puzzled about the scalloped circles, refer to *Stitches*, and see how to do line variations.)

Now for the fun applique. Do *not* cut out the applique. Pin the embroidered piece in place on the background material and put the whole thing in the hoop.

With the yellow thread and a medium zig zag, stitch all around the flower edge, using just enough stitches to secure it in place.

Without removing it from the hoop, take small scissors and trim away the surplus white sheer material close to the stitching.

Now put it under the needle again, and with wide zig zag, stitch over the cut edges, using the same stitch width and direction as was used for the embroidery. Move in and out a little as you go, blending the stitches and avoiding a ridge at the edge.

If you want to add an accent color at the edge, now is the time to do so. In fact, the applique could have been done with accent color, if that much color is desired.

It is exciting to see that the stitching at the edge causes the applique to raise, giving more depth to the embroidery. If you wish to accentuate a part of the embroidered area, simply stitch around that area and it becomes puffy within the stitched lines. For instance, the scalloped line circling the flower center could have been done *after* it was appliqued, making the center rounded. And what to do if you wish it was flat again? Simply add stitching wherever you want the applique to flatten.

Album Cover Designs

Scott and Nelson Barlow would never want a shirt that just *any* mother could embroider. Oh, no, theirs must be special and *different*. Therefore they presented their mom with two record album covers with pictures they liked and said *Go to it*. And go to it she did!

First, a piece of white polyester chiffon was laid over the desired picture, and the entire design was traced with a permanent ball point pen. When embroidery was begun, paper was placed under the hoop to stabilize the fabric and to make the design clearly visible.

Because of the intricate detail of the design, a great deal of the work was done in straight stitch. This is especially true of the faces.

In doing faces, embroider the features first, using a dark thread. Embroider the skin next with straight stitch and circular motion for a no-grainline appearance. (See *Stitches*.) The best colors we have found for flesh are DMC 948 for feminine and 712 for masculine. When the face is completed, go back and touch up the features with the dark thread, using straight stitch and going over it as many times as necessary.

After the bulk of the design is done, remove the paper from the back and pin the design into the shirt. Do not cut it out yet! With very narrow zig zag sew around the outside edge of the design. Trim the surplus chiffon away and you are ready for the finishing touches. The edges should now be stitched securely, matching stitch technique on each area of applique.

The main reason for doing the large or bulky work on the chiffon only is to prevent puckering the shirt. The fine details are done after it is appliqued.

Don't feel that it is necessary to cover all of the sheer fabric. That which shows adds another dimension and looks quite nice.

Crewel Embroidery
For Linda and Kathy
(See Color Section, pattern given)

These pictures are shown in full color in the center section, and the patterns are included in the packet.

Designed as a pair, or to be used separately, the models were made for our daughter-in-law, Linda, and for our niece, Kathy. Each chose her own thread colors and background material.

Linda wanted intense oranges and bright golds, with touches of red for accent. Greens would be bright avacado shades, and the bird of bold blue. Her choice of fabric was a linen-weave rayon of creamy beige.

Kathy chose natural linen, and soft colors of thread. The picture was to hang in her dining room, and she wanted blue to match her china. The greens would be light, bright shades, and the golds and yellows not too intense. Restraint here was the key, and that isn't easy for a gypsy like me.

General Instructions:
Choose a firmly woven fabric and cut it at least two inches larger than the frame you intend to use. Make sure there is enough material to accommodate the hoop all around. Center the design on the fabric and transfer with a hot iron.

Choose your thread colors and group them together. Determine where you want to use each color, and mark the area with matching crayon. You may change your mind as the work develops, but the crayons can be a help in getting started.

Now let's see about embroidering these pictures. We'll write about Kathy's first so I can send her finished picture off to Maryland. Poor Dear, she and Fred have moved into their new home and no doubt have a bare wall where this picture should hang.

Threads used were D.M.C. Machine Embroidery, sizes 30 and 50. The heavier #30 fills the large areas faster and builds texture more readily. Finer work goes better with #50.

Beginning with the tree trunk, three shades of brown were chosen. The very dark brown fills the lowest areas of the trunk, and afterward is used only for accenting branches.

Let me tell you how I planned the colors, and it may be of help to you some time. In the chosen threads there were three shades of yellow-to-orange, and one shade of gold, which would make up the larger flowers. These colors all combined well, but would become monotonous if combined in the same way on each flower. So I chose the brightest yellow, the orange, and the gold for the flower lowest on the tree, those at upper center, and upper right. These are the brightest colors, and by placing them that way, the eye is carried from bottom to top in a pleasing way.

The other large flowers use the light yellow instead of the bright shade, and they are just enough different to be quite pleasing.

Since blue was to predominate, the lower bird was done in all of the chosen shades of blue. The blue was picked up again in the three small flowers, using a medium and a light shade, with dark accent.

To carry the blue to the upper part of the picture, the butterfly was done in the palest shade, with a bit of medium blue, and a dark shade for accent.

Several shades of green were used for the upper bird, with softest blue-green for the breast, and light yellow-green on the throat area.

Leaves are done with the same family of greens as the bird. There was a question here: Should I choose a different family of greens for the leaves, and risk getting a too-busy effect, or use the same greens and maybe have the bird and leaves all look alike? Perhaps Kathy will tell us if we made the right decision.

Embroider The Picture:

Begin stitching anywhere you wish, but I usually start at the bottom, completing everything within the hoop before moving on. No, that needs a little justification; I invariably come back later and do more accenting, brighten up a flower, or maybe add more thread some place for texture. That's what makes it so much fun—knowing that you have all the freedom in the world to do whatever pleases you.

Let's take the picture a section at a time, and discuss details which may be of help to you.

The above photograph shows the lower portion of the picture. Look closely at the flower in the center. Can you tell whether the inner or the outer portions were worked first? Neither can I. The sequence of your work is usually a matter of choice. It is important, though that an area which overlays another should lie smoothly where the two parts join, so that the one appears to be on top.

It is important, too, that the stitches lie in the correct direction to indicate the grainline of petals, leaves, tree bark, feathers, etc.

The six dark spikes in the center of the flower are *tapered lazy daisies*. This was done on top of the already-embroidered petals. If you find it difficult to stitch over stitching, it should help to use a darning spring or embroidery foot. A finer needle might assist also.

The smaller flower to the right of the large one is a good example of using an accent color with small stitches to outline and set apart the different parts of an item. This is very well worth the effort on almost everything we do.

Now a look at the tree trunk. Whenever embroidering a heavily-textured area, consider using the heavier #30 thread.

Widest zig zag is called for here, and an uneven motion. For bark-like roughness, make your stitching deliberately lumpy, and unevenly spaced.

Add a shadow with a darker shade of thread, using medium-to-narrow stitch width. Let the dark stitches wander a little into the body of the embroidery.

Check the small details of the picture and you will find almost every part outlined with dark stitching. The illustration shows two pairs of lazy daisy leaves, one pair plain, the other accented. I'm addicted. Somehow, on crewel embroidery, any little area left un-accented seems to look naked.

Look at the next illustration. These are tail feathers. Widest zig zag and smooth motion make a nice effect. The one on the right has been accented, using straight stitch and an uneven motion, for a feathery appearance.

The body of the bird requires a finer stitch to give the appearance of the shorter, softer feathers. A medium zig zag does it, as shown at the left of the illustration below.

The breast feathers are finer still, and a straight stitch, worked in a side-to-side motion, (center), makes this effect.

On the head, or any place you might want a no-grainline effect, straight stitching is worked in a small circular motion to fill the area (right side of illustration).

The birds were really quite nice bits of embroidery before the line accenting went on, but look at the improvement it made!

One sure way to make a sparkling embroidered eye is to stitch it with gold or silver metallic thread, then surround it with tiny black stitches.

In working crewel designs on the machine, you need a good memory, or else keep referring to the pattern to find the details you covered up with your stitching. Then free-hand those details right over the previous stitching. Or better still, forget the pattern and ad lib the details.

Examples of this are the little "v's" on the bird, and the rib design on the larger flower petals.

It's ever so much fun to add your own touches to your embroidery. For instance, the four petals on the large flower had smooth edges in the beginning. However this did not quite please me, so when adding the accent thread, I used a jagged motion to make a feathery edge.

The leaf at the lower center of this portion was fun to do. One
thing about crewel—anything goes, so feel free when doing the details.
That zig zag line up the center of the leaf was easy enough to
free-hand, but you might think of something you would like even better.
And if it doesn't please you, consider stitching something else right
over the top of what you've already done.

Now let's get a bit playful with the flower on the right, and use
just the shape of it, but embroider it differently.

These are a couple of suggestions. For more ideas, sit at the
sewing machine, put your brain in gear, and see what comes out.

I love butterflies, and enjoy embroidering them. You can make them delicately colored, and subtly decorated, as in this one, or load them with sharply contrasting colors and flamboyant wing designs. Neat little feelers are appropriate for this picture, but another time you might make them long and graceful.

The main flower here is showy, and maybe a little bit busy. Say you are embroidering this flower, and after doing the criss-cross lines on the petals, you wish that you had left it plain. No problem. Simply thread up again with the petal color and re-embroider to cover the lines. Then go from there with whatever detail you would like.

Or maybe you would like to use a different technique than what the pattern lines suggest. Below are a couple of examples, but they are merely suggestions. Your imagination is the only thing which could limit the different ways that you could embroider each item.

Linda's Picture

Many of the techniques used here have been discussed in the preceding pages, and need not be repeated.

Beginning at the lower edge, let's see what we can do to be of help to you.

That heart-shaped *flower* at the right makes me a bit uncomfortable, because Linda didn't like it in the beginning. However, the thing was all designed and stamped, so we went ahead with it. Being so typically *crewel*, it fit nicely into the over-all theme.

Check the color plate in the center section, and let's see how this color scheme developed.

A rule of thumb says that once a color is introduced into a design, it should be used at least three times, being distributed in a pleasing way.

Since the intense orange was to predominate, it was used in the three small flowers, as well as being the outstanding color in the two large flowers.

Red and two shades of gold make the heart and the upper flower, with red and gold showing up in the strawberries also. The tiny berries held by the bird are of the same red.

Two shades of gold were used for the flower above the *heart*, and the one to the left of the bird's head. The gold in the larger flowers carries the thread of color through the design in a nice way.

Blue just had to be the color for the bird. Five shades are happily combined, with tiny areas of yellow for the beak, and the spots on the tail. Metallic gold is used subtly for the eye and for the slender plumes of the head dress.

The butterfly uses the second lightest shade of blue, and the same yellow as in the bird. He gets a gold eye, too.

Brightest avocado greens were needed to compliment the strong colors used in this picture.

Threads used were D.M.C. except for the intense orange, which is Mettler—a very good embroidery thread and luckily they had exactly the color I needed. I collect all kinds and colors, and they all have their place.

This flower departs a little from the pattern, but then my work nearly always does. I tried to follow the designs in this book for the sake of instruction, but there was a reason for changing this one.

In the beginning, the center was embroidered as designed, but it somehow looked pale and uninteresting. To improve it, I used rust colored thread, worked from center outward in a sunburst effect with narrow zig zag. A heavy French knot in the center completes it.

Look again at the color plate and notice the contrast between this flower and the upper one of the same colors. Notice that the lower one has the darker shades in the center, graduated to the light yellow on the outer portion, giving it a feeling of open airiness.

The upper flower has the heavier color on the outer part, giving it a heavy, bold appearance.

Sometimes we don't notice these things until long after they are completed, and then it becomes a learning experience. In this case I would have reversed the color schemes of the two flowers, for the sake of having the heavier color toward the bottom of the picture.

This lacy flower utilizes one of my favorite embroidery techniques—straight stitch embroidery. With no zig zag, there's no worry about turning the material for a proper grainline. With the needle going straight up and down, you're free as a bird to slide and glide anywhere you wish. Maybe this is one way to satisfy my long-time secret desire to be a dancer.

Now back to the embroidery. This flower was first done entirely in the darker shade of gold, and when finished it looked plain dull. No problem to put on the lighter shade and stitch an edge all around, then a few streaks through the petals for a much prettier flower.

In doing strawberries, cover the entire area first with heavy stitching, then move back toward the center, building more and more stitches for a rounded appearance.

If your machine balks at piling up stitches in this way, there are things you can do to help. Try using a stiff paper underneath, a darning spring on the needle, and a finer needle.

Add the berry seeds with a few small stitches placed at random in a natural way.

A row of dark thread in tiny stitches around the edge improves the rounded appearance of the berries.

Use these helps any time you want a rounded effect, on such items as grapes, cherries, flower centers, or whatever.

Helps for embroidering this bird are similar to those for the preceding picture.

This breast area was done with medium narrow zig zag, moving in a small circular motion for a no-grainline effect.

The lower neck area is made a little finer by narrowing the stitch a bit. The upper neck uses a finer stitch still, and the head is done with a straight stitch.

Just one change I would make in this bird. It is designed so that the upper edge of the wing, as it joins onto the body, is rounded, and appears to be on top of the body area. I wish I had embroidered it that way.

The flower at the left is interesting, in that it appears as a cluster of grapes. Of prime importance in embroidering a cluster of round objects is to run the stitches in a different direction on each one. That way, each will catch the light at a different angle, making them appear more natural.

A spot of lighter color gives a highlight to each round object, and a fine line of dark stitches around the edge adds to the rounded appearance.

This flower might be done in a variety of ways. You can also make changes as you go along, as I did.

In the beginning, the petals were embroidered as designed, using yellow for the body of the petals with a bold rim of orange at the edge. It looked harsh, so to soften it, the lighter orange was blended into both the yellow and the dark orange, and the shaded effect was lovely.

Also, the smaller petals which form a square within the flower, were embroidered with smooth edges, and seemed a little plain. Feathery stitching of rust at the edges set it apart, and it looked quite nice. The rust also accents the edges of the large petals.

The butterfly needed to be blue, but subtly colored to avoid detracting from the bird. The second lightest shade was used for the outer portion of the wings, with softest yellow-gold for the inner wing area. The metallic eye sparkles just a little. Outline the wings with the same dark blue as was used for the bird helps tie the design together.

On the two leaves shown above, an interesting technique was used to make them take a cupping shape. The side of the leaf with the smaller curves was done with straight stitching, giving those areas a fine, receding appearance. The side which makes a long, single curve is done with heavy, wide zig zag, carefully turning the material so that the stitches follow the curve all around. Tiny dark stitching at the edge accents the roundness, and you can almost visualize a little bug asleep in the leaf which curves upward.

The flower at the top combines light and dark gold with accents of red in such a way as to be light and bright. Heaviness here would put the picture out of balance.

All of the smaller leaves in the picture are medium green tapered lazy daisies, outlined with dark green. They would look just as well done in fill-in.

And this pretty well takes care of Linda's picture, and now it can hang on her wall where it belongs.

Let's Make Cutwork Fun
by Linda Zachary Goff

Since the 16th Century, cutwork has been one of the most elegant additions to embroidered clothing and linens. It was some time during the 16th Century that cutwork's popularity spread from Italy into France where the French developed their own style known as Richilieu. Richilieu is the filigree stitching or strings inside the cutout places.

Richilieu always adds beauty and sparkle to the embroidery, but it serves an important function also. Cutwork sometimes has curved or unusual shaped designs to be cut away and Richilieu helps these curves retain their shapes.

Traditionally, cutwork is a type of embroidery in which flowers, leaves, and abstract figures are surrounded by a heavy satin stitch; the background of these designs are then cut away. Traditional cutwork can be the most difficult because the cut out areas are usually large and irregular in shape. See Volume 2 of *Creative Machine Embroidery*, pp. 79, 81, and 82 for beautiful designs of this type.

Cutwork has always been limited to fabrics that do not fray or stretch, but if we are to use this art today, we must be able to remove these limitations. Today's fabrics can present some unique problems that if dealt with correctly, can make machine cutwork easier than ever. The key to success and ease with cutwork lies in stabilizing the cut edge so one can properly embroider these edges.

Let's now list three easy ways to stabilize our fabrics. One very simple way to stabilize is to lay a piece of paper under the cutwork edge and embroider this edge through the paper. Take care in choosing a paper that will tear away from the stitches easily without pulling the embroidery. Let us suggest a waxed paper, tracing or drafting paper, or light weight onion skin.

A second way to stabilize is to substitute a piece of nylon organdy for the paper under the hoops. The organdy remains sewn under the cutwork adding a shadowed effect. This shadowed effect furnishes privacy when cutwork is used on clothing. I just love the beautifully delicate look added by the organdy. I usually match the thread and organdy in color.

The third way to stabilize cutwork is the use of Richilieu.

Let us simplify cutwork and break from the traditional large background cutouts. We will try to reduce the cut areas for most of our work, but will show an interesting, new twist for large cut areas.

Machine Setting:

Feed dogs should be lowered or covered, presser foot off and bobbin tension set for normal sewing. The upper tension has two adjustments. For simple cutwork the tension is loosened the same amount as for regular embroidery. When constructing the Richilieu bars, it is more easily accomplished with a slightly tighter tension.

Thread:

Always be careful in cutwork to match the color of thread on the top of the machine and in the bobbin. By using the colored, 50 weight thread in the bobbin, you will get a better tension for the Richilieu bars. A contrasting color in the bobbin case always shows in your work when embroidering the cut edges and Richilieu.

Darning Spring:

Many times the darning spring is helpful for handling polyester fabrics and in getting smooth embroidery along the cut edges of other fabrics. Be alert to the possibility that the spring will snag in the Richilieu stitching. We don't know of any solution except to be patient, and on fabrics needing a spring, use Richilieu as little as possible.

Cutwork Shapes:

As one looks through the pattern books searching for possible cutwork patterns, we find this to be a bit difficult since the standard pattern companies are not currently publishing many patterns specifically for cutwork. Let us now become familiar with certain shapes so we can adapt standard patterns for our use in cutwork.

Pig's Eye:

Probably the easiest shape and many times the smallest is the *pig's eye*. It is so ideal for cutwork because we can simply glide around the design with the satin stitches across the ends of the points, thus adding stability.

Method:

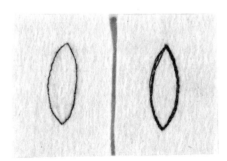

Straight stitch (no zig zag) around the entire design.

Then retrace your stitching line two more times for a total of three times. Try to make rows 2 and 3 just on top of stitching row 1; however, don't fret too much if the stitching is not exact as now is not too critical a time for perfect work as it will be covered with beautiful stitching later.

Now cut out the center. Be very careful to cut close to your stitching. Cutting is one of the most critical steps in cutwork because the degree of difficulty of neatly embroidering the edges is so greatly increased if we have ragged, uneven cutting.

On fabrics that fray, it is almost impossible to neatly satin stitch the cutwork unless cutting is done *extremely* close to the prestitching. Take care not to cut the prestitching.

Set the zig zag to a medium width. Stitch around the design one time quickly. Take care to let the needle drop well into the fabric and just barely into the cut area.

It is now that paper or organdy is placed under the hoops to stabilize the stitching area.

Again stitch around the *pig's eye*. This time evenly satin stitch the cut edge exactly retracing the first stitches. Notice that the stitching crosses the pointed ends.

The *pig's eye* is often found in floral designs indicating small leaves or flower petals. Keeping this shape small makes it easier than other usually larger ones.

Diamond:

Let us expand the *pig's eye* now, and call the next shape the *diamond* so we can differentiate between the two shapes. The *diamond* is always pointed on both ends, but is much larger in most pattern designs. The *diamond* is the shape of most large leaves.

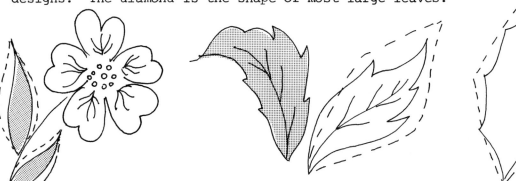

There is more character and interest to the *diamond*. This is a perfect place to use Richilieu to add the veins of the leaf.

Teardrop:

The next shape we will consider is the teardrop. It is pointed on one end and rounded on the other. This shape takes a bit more effort as we must pivot around the curved end keeping the stitches wide around the curve. It is probably the most difficult of all the shapes. A little patience in working teardrops and they will become a favorite and one of the most elegant.

Many leaves can be considered as *teardrops*.

Some flowers also duplicate this shape.

The teardrop is used frequently in the throat of flowers, but we can expand the teardrop to include an entire bud. Try the organdy shadowing underneath the design when cutting out an entire bud or flower petal.

Cutwork is designated by shaded areas.

Let your imagination run wild now as you look through pattern books. Enjoy cutwork and its many uses. Use cutwork in clothing or linens, in casual or very dressy clothing.

Method — Teardrop:

Stitch all around the teardrop three times with a straight stitch (no zig zag).

Very carefully cut out the center fabric taking great care to cut close to the stitching rows, but not to cut the thread.

Set a medium zig zag. Plan to embroider this shape with only one stitching row around. We must pivot around the curve. As you approach the curve, stop with the needle down in the fabric. Turn the hoops just a little bit. Take a few more stitches. Again stop with the needle down in the fabric, and continue around the rest of the curve and back to the top.

Shelley's Apron
(See color section for pattern)

Isn't Shelley's apron an adorable cutwork effect? This just may become one of our favorites because of its simplicity and speed. I just love this casual change from the many elegant ideas.

Any very sturdy, nonfraying fabric will take these large cutouts. We tried the suede cloth and polyester double knit with great success.

Machine Setting:
A darning spring on the needle is a must to prevent rolling of the cut edges. Use a size 70 or size 11 needle and 50 weight machine embroidery thread, both top and bobbin. Tension is adjusted to the normal loosened setting for embroidery.

Method:
Trace your pattern onto light weight onion skin or artist's tracing paper. Pin the paper in place on top of the fabric and put both into the hoops. Lay a sheet of type or notebook paper under the hoops.

With a narrow zig zag, sew around your design only one time. Let this stitching be fairly sketchy so as not to cut the paper underneath too much.

Cut out the fabric cutting only the fabric, but leaving the paper still in place behind the design. This paper controls these large cut areas so no stretching or rolling occurs.

Then using a medium wide zig zag, glide around the design only one time for the final embroidery, as too many stitches cause the large cut areas to ripple.

I know you will thoroughly enjoy this simple, quick and striking type of cutwork.

Perky Peacock
(See color section, pattern given)

As a change from the usual flowers, Gail designed this clever peacock for cutwork. See the completed model in the color section. Organdy was added for a shadowed effect, and to help control fraying of the fabric.

Special Technique:

Since we are using a linen-like woven material, the rows of prestitching will be done with a narrow zig zag instead of straight stitching.

Method:

1. *Prestitching*—Zig zag one time around with a narrow stitch.

2. Zig zag a second time around with a narrow stitch.

3. *Cut*—Cut very close to stitching lines.

4. *Stabilize*—Lay organdy under hoops behind the cut out. Stitch one time around using medium zig zag.

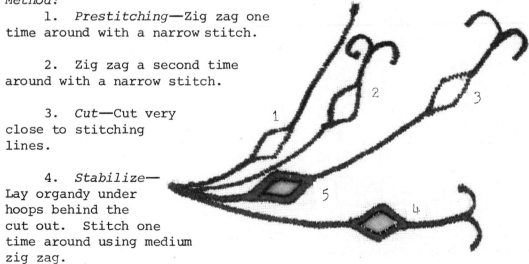

5. *Embroidery*—Final embroidery
second time around with medium stitch.

Now let us look at the large areas of Richilieu on the wings.

Method:
Stitch around the wing two times with a narrow zig zag to stabilize
the outer edge.

Begin to cut out the wing from one end and
one side.

The Richilieu design should be sketched
onto a light weight onion skin paper. This
paper is then placed exactly under the cut
areas.

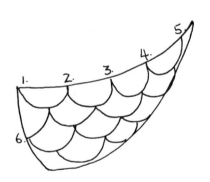

With a very sketchy narrow zig zag,
stitch through the paper on the drawn lines.
The bars are then added a little at a time as
more fabric is cut away until the entire wing
is completed.

Anchor the stitching into the fabric at
position #1 and stitch across the paper to
anchor again at position #2. Stitch back and forth again forming a
series of four strings. In some places
heavier Richilieu is desired and this is
achieved using six strings. To obtain
extremely heavy Richilieu use four
strings and 30 weight machine embroidery
thread.

Progress to the next higher numbers
in the same manner stopping at the end of
each row to embroider that row of strings.

Embroider the strings very carefully with a medium width zig zag.
You will probably find this intricate Richilieu takes much patience
and a bit of practice. Cover the strings closely going one time over
them. A slightly tighter tension will make this process much easier.

Caution—Do not use too heavy a paper for the Richilieu pattern
under the cut area or the paper will not cut away from the stitching
easily.

Refer to Volume 2 of *Creative Machine Embroidery,* pp. 76-81 for
patterns of large Richilieu areas.

Fantasyland Castle
(See color section, no pattern given)

Abstract designs are so popular today suggesting Indian motifs as well as fantasy designs. Our Fantasyland Castle has been such a thrill for our darling little Sally. The shadowed cut work and Richilieu in the small windows gives the illusion of cracked window panes. Let this abstract art stimulate your imagination. Just apply the shapes mentioned and experiment to see how many innovations you can come up with.

As we began to applique the lace pieces in their respective places, a very delicate appearance formed. To compliment this look, we decided to try for small Richilieu.

Since this dress is made from cotton velveteen, the fabric presented no problems of fraying or stretching. We used standard cutwork techniques.

Method:

The diamond shape is worked using the same techniques as the *pig's eye*. Surround the window with one line of straight stitching (no zig zag).

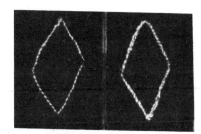

Then repeat all around the design with two more rows of straight stitching.

Now that the edges are stabilized, it is time to cut the inside of the design out. Remember to cut very carefully.

Small Richilieu is easily accomplished by anchoring the thread well into the fabric at position #1. Then sew to position #2 and back again to position #1, forming only two strings.

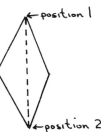

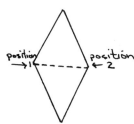

With a stitch that is slightly smaller than a medium zig zag, embroider the strings. Skip across the string one time very lightly, then a second time for a smooth Richilieu bar. Remember a tighter-than-normal tension should be used while working on the bars.

You are ready now to finish the window edge. Under your hoops lay a piece of nylon organdy, then put a spring on the needle to help control the velveteen nap. Set the zig zag on medium width and glide around the edges quickly one time. Be sure the stitch width lays across the point of the diamond.

Retrace your stitching line with a second satin stitch; this time watch for quality. Get all cut threads sewn under and using closely packed stitches.

The castle doorway presents several interesting ideas. Encircle the door with three rows of straight stitching.

Then begin to cut from the lower right corner upwards about one-third the way up and across to the left, then upwards again.

Slip a piece of paper under the doorway. On the paper there should be a drawn plan of the Richilieu placement. Actually sew the strings through the paper. Anchor the thread at position #1 and sew across the opening to position #2 and back to position #1 using a very narrow zig zag.

Cut upwards again and add more strings which will hold the shape of the doorway. You will find this straight Richilieu much easier than the curved ones on the peacock.

When all Richilieu is in place, carefully embroider the strings with a medium zig zag.

Lay a piece of organdy under the hoops to shadow the doorway. Quickly sew around the doorway edge to stabilize it to the organdy. Then retrace the prestitching with a final, smooth embroidery.

Study the close-up on the following page to clarify any questions you might have on this.

95

Mother's Christmas Present
(See Color Section, pattern given)

Creating this lovely blouse has been lots of fun because it is for someone so special. The pattern used was adapted from Volume 2 of *Creative Machine Embroidery*, p. 80, to contain smaller areas of cutwork and retain a very simple design.

The white shirting was chosen because it is a fabric all of us wear so often. Woven fabrics such as this must be handled with a little more care because they fray so readily. A simple way to control the fraying is to use a lightweight bondable interfacing on the under side of the cloth. A woven interfacing will accept the embroidery with ease whereas a non-woven one stabilizes the fabric too much and more puckering around the embroidery results. The interfacing should remain in place after the garment is embroidered to add durability to the cutwork.

Secondly, in handling a woven material, may we suggest that you always replace the straight stitching three times around the design with two times around using a narrow zig zag. This gives a wider stitching area, further stabilizing the edge to be cut.

Thirdly, a darning spring aids greatly in getting a smoothly embroidered edge on the cutwork and a heavy paper needs to be held under the hoops to stabilize edges and prevent puckering.

Method:

Richilieu is added on the curved lines to hold the curve in place so it would not roll, but also because it is so beautiful.

Stitch around the design edge two times with a narrow zig zag. Cut away fabric carefully. With a straight stitch anchor the thread well into the fabric at position #1. Stitch to position #2 and back to position #1, then again to position #2 and end at position #1. This has just constructed a heavier bar with four strings to strengthen the large curves.

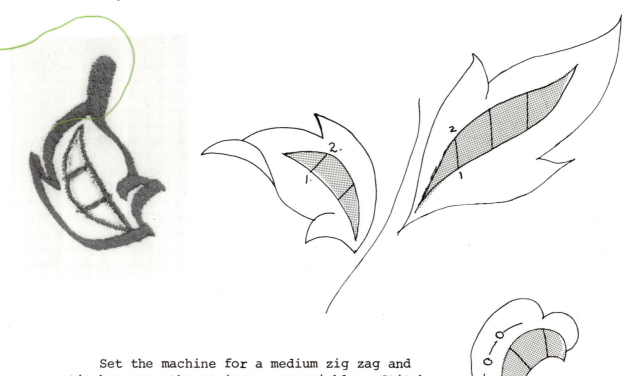

Set the machine for a medium zig zag and stitch across the strings once quickly. Stitch over the Richilieu a second time for a smoother bar. Remember, a slightly tighter tension helps give an evenly embroidered bar. If the tension is too loose there are bumps and loops formed as you cross the bar.

To embroider the cutwork edges, treat this shape as a *pig's eye* except on the widely curved side where we must pivot the curve as described on the teardrop.

Midnight Sparkle
(See color section, pattern given)

Every aspect of designing this dress was carefully considered to present many new challenges. It is made of royal blue Qiana—royal blue because it is my favorite color, and Qiana because it is a very special, elegant fabric of today. Needless to say, this dress has been the most complicated and challenging of all these projects.

The embroidery design for this dress is simplified to specifically suit the elegance of the dress. The sleeve design is an adaptation of the one in Volume 2, *Creative Machine Embroidery*, p. 78. The neckline was drawn to fit the dress using the same flowers and leaves, but simplified slightly.

It is lots of fun to create new patterns from existing ones. You will be pleased to find it easier than you may think. Just try it once.

Machine Setting:
A darning spring is a must for this or any other knit fabric. A ball point needle is highly recommended, but not a necessity. Feed dogs must be down to avoid snagging the under side of the knit.

Tension:
When working on knits of any kind, but specifically on the softer ones, use a scrap of the material to test for the perfect tension for that material. For this dress, the top tension was adjusted as for regular embroidery. Richilieu was constructed with a slightly tighter top tension. The bobbin tension should be loosened enough so puckering of the fabric does not occur.

Caution:
There seems to be only one area for a word of caution concerning knits and cutwork. When putting the fabric into the hoops, take great care to keep the crosswise and lengthwise stretches evenly firm. *Do not* stretch either onto the bias or rippling occurs. Generally, we do not even want to stretch the knit at all while in the hoops. Also, be sure there aren't any bubbles in the fabric to sew into puckers. We just want the fabric firmly in the hoops, but not stretched.

Stabilize:

Now let us emphasize the importance of stabilizing this soft knit while sewing. We used sheer applique in the flowers. Sheer applique is one of my most favorite of all the embroidery techniques because it is such a delicate look. Sheer applique is the application of a sheer fabric such as nylon organdy to another material to add color and interest.

Refer to Volume 2 of *Creative Machine Embroidery*, pp. 91-104 for more details on using sheer applique. The sheer applique was particularly helpful on my blue dress because it stabilized the knit from the top side.

On every stitch taken during this embroidery, there was light weight onion skin paper under the hoops to stabilize the fabric from underneath.

Organdy was used again under the neckline cutwork to add privacy, but also to stabilize the knit. Don't you think it is beautiful too?

Method:

I traced the flowers onto the organdy with a regular pencil. The flowers were then placed on top of the blue Qiana and paper placed under the hoops. I then used a medium wide stitch to embroider the flower edges. Oh, what a fast pattern transfer technique!

For the remaining leaves and stems, the patterns of these were drawn onto tracing paper. The paper was then put on top of the yoke both for pattern transferring and stabilizing. Using a straight stitch, sew through the paper outlining the designs. The paper is then easily pulled away from the stitching. We are left with the neckline pattern perfectly transferred, and areas to be cut out for cutwork already prestitched. On a fabric as delicate as the Qiana, only one time around for prestitching is enough.

Cut out the areas to be done in cutwork while the material is still in the hoops. Cut very carefully. It is at this point that you will know whether or not you put the fabric into the hoops correctly. If you did it right, the cut work retains its shape. But if you stretched the fabric, the cut area gets a new shape once the cutting begins.

Next, construct small Richilieu made with only two strings to keep it small and delicate. Embroider these strings using a medium zig zag.

Embroider the edges of the cutwork stabilizing with paper under the hoops using a medium width stitch.

Wasn't that fun and easy too? I hope you will find many uses for cutwork on formal clothing and even wedding dresses. It is a beautiful and delicate type of embroidery.

100

Fine Embroidery
Mats For Your Treasured Photos
(See color section, patterns given.)

We thought this a fun and beneficial way to bring into this book some helps on doing fine embroidery. Besides we love to show off our cute grandchildren. Whether or not you ever do a picture mat, you will likely find some helps here for doing the things you wish.

Each mat was designed with a particular child in mind, so we have a variety. Colors were chosen to correspond with the child's coloring and clothing, so your colors would no doubt be different. A little explanation of why some things were done the way they were may be of benefit to you.

The designs were stamped onto off-white rayon fabric of linen-like weave. The embroidery was done and pressed, then each picture was mounted and framed. The photos were cut to size and attached with rubber cement, and a strand of gold yarn applied at the edge with white glue. Now that sounds just too simple, but each step will be fully explained in the chapter following this one.

Embroidering fine designs is not as difficult as it appears to be. Just think small and work patiently. If you make up your mind that you want to do it, you can.

Decide how much embroidery you want on your item. You know, you can take a design and load it with heavy stitching and it will appear quite different from the same design worked in thin embroidery. I prefer the heavy look, but the choice is yours to make.

Starting at the top left we will give helps on each design. Better read them all—you may find just the tips you need for doing your other projects too.

Jennifer's picture has a flowered background so we hesitated to use anything floral on her mat. Somehow the teddy bears seemed just right for her. On the pattern the bears are wearing bow ties, but we changed them to girlish ribbon bows while doing the embroidery.

The bears are done in straight stitch fill-in, gliding the material so that the needle *draws* each part of the design. If this seems difficult, refer to *Straight Stitch for Contours* on page 10 in the Glossary.

In doing the upright bears a series of oval shaped lines forms the feet. The spots on the paws and the ears are done in the same way. The ears use a little out-and-back motion for a fuzzy effect. The heads on these tall bears are done with circular lines beginning at the outer edge and spiraling the stitching toward the center.

In doing the body, think of the direction the fur would grow on an animal and shape the stitching lines accordingly.

One thing we found for sure in doing the sixteen little bear heads was that they are easier to do if you fill in the faces completely first, then ad lib the features over this stitching.

Colors used were brown a little darker than Jennifer's hair and coral pink to blend with her facial tones and the flowers in the background.

Jason being the only boy just had to have a variety of boyish things about him. The artist came up with a cute combination, making our job easy.

One problem here was avoiding the use of too many colors. Check the color section on this.

Green was no problem, as we had decided to use the same light and dark yellow-green for all of the pictures.

Turquoise blue brings out the color of Jason's eyes and blends nicely with his shirt.

The elephants of course must be pink, the lion gold, and the ducks light orange. It needed a lot of red, and by putting it on the wheels at the bottom, clowns at the sides, and birds at the top, it makes the red predominant. Bits of gold metallic were used for some of the eyes and the details on the clowns.

Everything in this picture was done in straight stitch except the flowers, stems and leaves.

Melanie's salmon colored dress called for shades of salmon thread to match. These are D.M.C. numbers 349, 350 and 353, and they look very pretty here.

A lot of narrow and medium zig zag was used in embroidering this one. The flowers should be heavy, which ordinarily calls for wide zig zag. However, this would be difficult because of the small size of the flowers. A narrow stitch is much easier to control in small areas, and by using this and going over it several times, the desired result was achieved. Outlining of the flowers was avoided because it might make the whole thing look too busy. The soft yellow French knot center was all that was needed.

Leaves are of heavy fill-in, with accents and stems of very narrow satin stitch.

The butterflies are of bright yellow-gold fill-in with bodies and accents of #349 salmon.

Starting at the lower left with *Kristy*, we find this mat an interesting grouping of things kids like. This one was the most difficult in choosing colors and deciding what should go where.

Because of Kristy's blue eyes and the background of the same color, we must have lots of blue in the design. D.M.C. 806 and 807 matched nicely, and these were used abundantly without seeming to overdo it.

Red must be used generously, and the bird, the strawberry, and the ladybug were naturals for this color. Some flowers and small details were done in red, and in finishing the design we cheated and added some small details in red which are not in the pattern at all.

Lots of yellow and dark gold finish the design, along with the same greens as in the other pictures.

ᕙᕗᕙᕗᕙᕗᕙᕗᕙᕗᕙᕗᕙᕗ

Lori looks so grown up in this photo that her mat had to be a bit dressy. We think the design is quite classic and would do justice to the most sophisticated picture.

We chose dark red and two shades of pink to pick up the colors in Lori's dress and skin tones. The flowers are simple fill-in with bright yellow French knot centers. Leaves are tapered lazy daisy, and stems are narrow satin stitch.

ᕙᕗᕙᕗᕙᕗᕙᕗᕙᕗᕙᕗᕙᕗ

The lavender of *Shalane's* dress was easy to complement with lavender, purple and pink threads. The greens are the right shades to tie it all together, and the soft yellow of the centers is in keeping with the rest.

Fill-in is used for the leaves and flowers, except those done in tapered lazy daisy. Purple French knots make the small dots, with the larger knots done in lavender and pink.

ᕙᕗᕙᕗᕙᕗᕙᕗᕙᕗᕙᕗᕙᕗ

The mat with the rosebuds is a lovely design, and versatile to use. It was chosen for *Shannon's* picture because her pink dress would match the roses.

A funny thing happened in doing this. The design was embroidered at night, and in the artificial light the pinks seemed to match. When morning came and the natural light showed the thread to be the wrong shade, we had to figure a way to fix it.

This was done by threading up with pink to match the dress, and using straight stitches to partially cover the first stitching. The blending of the two shades is quite pleasing, and it accomplishes the goal.

You will find it possible to cover mistakes easily in doing Machine Embroidery, and this is one more reason to let yourself go so that all of your creative talents can surface.

Press Your Embroidery

Correct pressing makes such a difference in your finished work that it must not be neglected.

Equipment is not hard to come by. A good iron with automatic heat control is a must. This may be either a standard or a steam iron. I prefer the standard as it has no vents in the bottom to drag over the embroidery.

You will also need several thicknesses of soft cloth. Keep this near my ironing board for this purpose, and they go in the laundry occasionally to keep them soft.

Another required item is a can of spray fabric finish, or a spray bottle of water.

Method:
Turn the iron to the correct setting for the fabric you are using. Lay four or more thicknesses of soft material on the ironing board and place the embroidered piece face down on this. Spray until the fabric is quite damp, then begin to press.

Put plenty of pressure on the iron. As the heat and the moisture generate steam, the fabric and stitching relax, letting the iron press the embroidery down into the soft fabric. This leaves the embroidered material lying flat so that the iron can do a good job of smoothing it and removing any puckers.

This may need to be repeated again, and you may need to press it from different directions to get it entirely smooth. This is so worth whatever effort it takes, so *persevere* until you are pleased with the results.

Mount Your Embroidery For Framing

The first thing to do is to obtain the frame you want to use—
this even before the embroidery is started. Then get a mounting board
cut to fit the frame. This may be stiff cardboard, thin plywood, or
paneling, etc.

Press the embroidered piece thoroughly and center it on the
mounting board. Now turn each corner of the embroidered fabric back
and mark it with pencil at the corner of the board.

Lay the embroidery face down and leave it while you prepare the
board.

You will need a can of spray adhesive, and this may be purchased
at a hardware store. Read the label and make sure that it says it may
be used on fabric, paper, wood, etc.

Spread newspapers on the floor, table or other area, preferably
in the fresh air. Now lay the mounting board in the center of the
paper and spray thoroughly with the adhesive. You want it to appear
all bubbly without making puddles.

Pick the board up by the edges and position it glue side down over
the embroidered piece, lining up the marked corners. Drop the board in
place and immediately turn it over. Work quickly to get every little
part of the fabric pressed against the glue by running your fingertips
close to the stitching. Use an orangewood stick or other blunt object
for hard-to-reach places. The glue sets up fast, so if your board
placement is not correct the first time, lift quickly and try again.

With the fabric glued securely in place, trim the surplus away
close to the cardboard. It is now ready to slip into the frame.

In order to keep your spray can in working condition, read the
label and do as it says. If you fail to clean the nozzle as directed,
it will soon be plugged and will refuse to work.

Yarn Stitchery

Introduction:

Yarn work offers a wide range of possibilities when using the sewing machine. You may do anything from large, bold designs with the bulkiest yarns, to intricate and delicate work with gossamer threads.

Having a variety of colors and textures of yarn on hand would be of great benefit to you. Let your family and friends know that you are collecting these and they will likely want to help. Anything which will bend is usable if the needle will pierce it or jump over it.

When working on items to be laundered frequently, such as children's clothing, use synthetic yarns, or those you know will wash.

The Glossary of Yarn Stitches will be referred to frequently in the instructions. You will find many worthwhile helps there, but we do not pretend to have all of the stitches represented because many have not yet been invented. You will no doubt come up with a few of your own as you explore the use of this medium.

You will find that the simple secret in doing yarn work is in placing the yarn, then stitching it down with nylon *invisible* thread (see *Sources*). The bobbin thread may be either embroidery or regular sewing thread. If the back of the stitched item will not be seen when in use, you may want to use up all of your half-empty bobbins here.

Almost any fabric adapts well for yarn work. Depending on its use, choose upholstery fabrics, canvas, burlap, linen, or linen-like weaves, denim, wearing apparel, etc. For your beginning work use a firm fabric.

The yarn designs in this book are all new, and the finished models are shown in color. The valance design is a collection of a lot of fun things, and you will find them all as transfer patterns in the packet.

The afghan design is not given as a transfer pattern, but instructions and illustrations are clear and concise so that you may duplicate or adapt this for your own use.

Remember as you work that Yarn Stitchery is a creative venture, and not just a way of copying something. Experiment with it to find out what you can do, then play it to the hilt. Yarn Stitchery on the machine is an art of its own, and we may go any direction we choose in exploring the many creative possibilities.

Set Up The Machine:

Remove presser foot, put feed dogs out of action. No darning foot or spring is needed. Use a fine needle and straight stitch.

Thread up with invisible thread. On the bobbin use either machine embroidery or regular thread.

Check tensions. Regular tension on the bobbon, top tension loosened enough that the stitch is relaxed and does not distort the yarn.

No hoop is needed for this work. Choose a firm fabric for your practice.

Begin Your Practice:

Lay a length of yarn on your practice material. Try stitching along the edge of the yarn, guiding the fabric so that the needle barely catches into the yarn fibers. After the stitching, the yarn should roll back over the stitches, making them completely invisible.

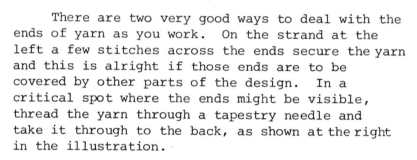

There are two very good ways to deal with the ends of yarn as you work. On the strand at the left a few stitches across the ends secure the yarn and this is alright if those ends are to be covered by other parts of the design. In a critical spot where the ends might be visible, thread the yarn through a tapestry needle and take it through to the back, as shown at the right in the illustration.

Curved lines are no more difficult than are straight ones. Try making circles, leaf shapes, even writing your name with yarn, just to get the feel of taking the yarn in different directions.

When making a point such as the tip of the leaf, stitch across the yarn and back, adjust the twist of the yarn, then proceed down the other side of the leaf. It is usually neater to keep the stitching on the inside of the design. At the lower end of the leaf, again stitch over the yarn and take the line on up to form the vein. At the end of the vein is a good example of a need to take the yarn through to the back of the fabric.

At this point of learning yarn work, the best help you can get is in playing with it until you feel quite comfortable in handling this technique. Try the stitches in the following Glossary.

Glossary of Yarn Stitches

Fasten the Yarn:

  If you are working in an area where the end of the stitching will be hidden by other stitching later, simply stitch across and back a couple of times to secure it. If in a critical place where the end will show, thread the yarn into a tapestry needle and take it through to the back.

Simple Outline:

  Lay the yarn on the line in a relaxed way, and guide the fabric under the needle so that the stitches barely catch into the fiber of the yarn.

  Keep the line continuous wherever possible in order to avoid excessive yarn ends. For instance, you may outline the leaf, then go out and back on the stem and finally do the veins of the leaf without cutting the yarn.

Flat Loops:

  This is a frequently used variation of the simple outline. Make it by flipping a small loop at intervals as desired, stitching just where the yarn crosses itself as it makes the loop.

  To keep the loops even and flat against the fabric, be sure to stitch on the same side of the yarn as the loops will be.

  A pair of tweezers is helpful in handling the yarn in this and many other areas.

Thorny Stem:

  This stitch is used to good advantage in making stems and leaves and may be varied from bold to delicate depending on thickness of the yarn used and the way you handle it.

  To use this technique fasten the yarn. Stitch downward on the line for a short distance, then secure the yarn by stitching across and back over it. Make a jog in the line by bringing the yarn upward and a little to the left. Stitch upward a very short distance, then across the yarn and back. Bring the yarn downward again and stitch along it for the same distance as above. Keep repeating this process for the desired line.

Chain Stitch and Variation:
       The chain stitch with its variations is used
often for stems, outlines, fill-in, etc.

       Make it with two strands of yarn. Fasten
them together on the fabric and lay one over the
other forming a chain link of the desired size.
Stitch across the yarn where the strands overlap.
Form another chain by crossing one over the other,
then stitch again. Continue for the desired outline.

       If an added detail is desired, lay another
strand of yarn along the center of the finished
chain and stitch in place. The first time I used
this was on a large stitchery on which all of the
stems had been done in bold chain stitch. The
light color of the background fabric showing
through all of those chain links made an
undesirable busy appearance. An overlay added
to the chain stitch stems made a remarkable
difference.

Twist Stitch:
       A nice change from the chain stitch is the
twist. This is made by simply overlapping the
strands closely with no open link in the center.
The twist may be any size, depending on the size
of yarn used.

       This stitch was used to good advantage in
doing the *Floral Afghan*. Having done the stems
in the thorny stem stitch, the risk of making the
whole thing too busy was very real. Fearing that
the chain stitch would add to the busyness, the
twist stitch was used instead, with happy results.

Fill-In Stitch:
       This is easier to do than you might think.
It is simply a continuation of *Simple Outline*,
making row on row until you have the desired area
filled.

       Depending on the yarn used, you may achieve
endless interesting effects. This stitch was used
in a number of different ways in doing the
valance, and this will be discussed fully in that
chapter.

Satin Stitch:

A simple satin stitch is intended to be rather smooth and plain, and is used to fill a border, a leaf or flower shape, etc.

To learn how to do this stitch, first draw on your fabric two parallel lines about an inch apart. 1) Lay the end of the yarn across the line on the left and stitch in place. 2) Now quickly stitch across to the line on the right, then take the yarn over to the right and stitch it where it lies across the line. 3) Now stitch back to the left line. As you prepare to take the yarn over to the left line, notice that it folds right over the stitches you made previously. This avoids having any machine stitches showing, and assures a smooth satin stitch. 4) Now take the yarn to the left line, stitch over it, stitch back to the right side, take the yarn to the right and stitch it down, and keep this going until you have filled the border.

Take care to let the yarn lie gently relaxed as you work, and watch to maintain the natural *twist* of the yarn fibers.

Flip Satin Stitch:

This is made nearly like the satin stitch above, except for the *flip* we incorporate which makes a definite texture.

Begin with Step 1 the same as above. On Step 2 instead of simply laying the yarn directly across, bring it upward and then across, twisting it a bit so that it makes a definite hump above the stitching. Let it be quite lax as you stitch it on the line at the right side.

On Step 3, use a small tool such as a screw driver or tweezers to form the yarn into a little hump above the stitching as you prepare to take it back to the left side. Now lay it on the left line and stitch over it, and you will see that a *figure 8* has been formed.

111

Repeat this process from left to right and right to left, keeping the loops close together so that they support one another.

Leaf of Flip Satin:
Draw a leaf shape onto your fabric. Begin at the wider end and work from side to side, stitching on the line each time as you follow the contour.

On reaching the tip of the leaf make a small loop pointing upward and stitch in place. Leave a length of yarn to thread into a tapestry needle and work the end back into the leaf an inch or so, then clip off the excess.

Notice that the stitches have formed a vein line down the center of the leaf. You may leave it this way, or take a line of stitching along the vein line. Accentuate it further if you wish by adding a line of fine yarn.

Rotating Flip:
This stitch, when mastered, is most elegant. It makes lovely petals, leaves, rose buds, flower centers, etc. Let us take it a step at a time and see how to do it.

Step 1. Draw a petal shape on your fabric. Lay the end of yarn inside the petal near the right edge. Stitch back and forth across the yarn where it crosses the upper line. We will rotate the yarn in a clockwise direction. Step 2. With the right hand give the yarn a little twist and draw it downward. Lay the yarn across the lower line and stitch back and forth on the line to anchor it. Now stitch upward to the top line. Step 3. Now bring the yarn up, stitch across it on the upper line, then stitch downward to the lower line. Step 4. Again give the yarn a little twist and a downward flip, and lay it across the lower line. Stitch in place. Step 5. Continue in this manner to complete the petal.

112

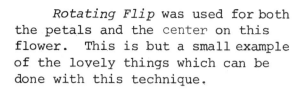

Rotating Flip was used for both the petals and the center on this flower. This is but a small example of the lovely things which can be done with this technique.

Be on the lookout for ideas and designs which appeal to you. This rotating flip was adapted from a design on a straw bag which was made in the Orient. Work with it until it becomes comfortable, then you may incorporate it into almost any design.

The tiny *Rosebud* is merely suggestive of one more shape you might try using the rotating flip. If it had a calyx and a stem, it would be believable. We did some tiny ones in a lustrous rayon cord once, and they were lovely.

Lazy Daisy:

Draw a daisy with five or more petals. The more brief the drawing, the more freedom you will have in forming the design with your yarn, i.e., straight lines instead of petal loops.

Step 1. At the base of one of the petals on the left, fasten the end of the yarn with a few straight stitches (using invisible thread, of course). Run a line of stitching to the outer tip of the petal, without catching into the yarn. With the needle in the material bring the yarn out and around it, forming the rounded tip of the petal. Stitch over the yarn, then back to the base of the petal, without catching the yarn.

Step 2. Bring the yarn back to the base of the petal and secure it with a few straight stitches.

Step 3. Lift the yarn out of the way and stitch to the tip of the next lower petal. Stop with the needle in the material as before and bring the yarn around it. Stitch over the yarn and back to the center. Proceed in this manner until all of the petals are done.

Lifted Loops:

This is an easy and versatile way to make flower centers, fluffy animals, doll hair, fill in a background, or even a rug. Here is a simple way to begin.

Step 1. Stitch the center of a strand of yarn to the fabric.

Step 2. Hold the strands firmly with the left hand at the left of the needle. Using a slender tool such as a small screw driver, lift both strands and pull to the right. The further you pull, the longer the loops will be. Stitch twice across the base of the loops and remove the tool.

Step 3. Lift the yarn again to form more loops, and stitch across to anchor. Continue in this way until the desired area is filled. Use more strands for faster fill-in.

Fringe Loops:

A simple hairpin-shaped wire frame with the closed end bent upward can help you make fringe quickly and easily. (See *Sources*.) With this fringe you may make an endless number of lovely things.

Fringe is made simply by wrapping the yarn on the frame, then stitching just inside the wire on one side. By holding the closed end to the right as you stitch, the yarn may be wrapped, stitched, and removed from the open end at the left.

Fringe may be made by the yard for use on pillows, clothing, etc. Or make it a few inches at a time as needed for flowers or other items on your stitcheries.

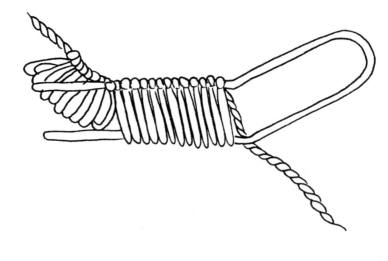

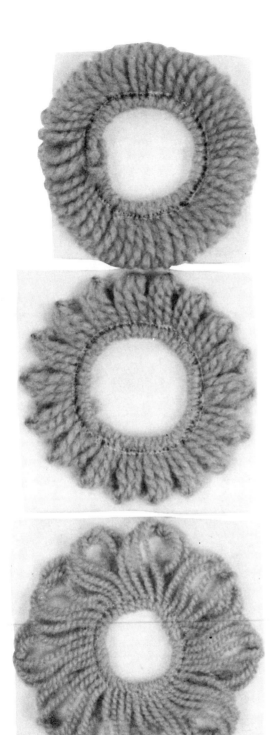

Fringe Flowers:

Take a piece of finished fringe and form it into a circle on your fabric. Stitch in place, letting the stitches fall directly over the stitches of the fringe. You are now ready to finish the flower in whatever way you choose.

A very pretty flower is fashioned by gathering the fringe loops into clusters to form petals. A tapestry needle is threaded with yarn, either to match or contrast, and is brought through from the back. The desired number of loops are picked up, then the yarn taken to the back again, ready for the next stitch. On this sample the petals each contain three loops.

A larger frame makes wider fringe. The finer yarn gives a lacy appearance, letting the background material show through. Five loops were used for each petal.

There are many interesting variations possible in making fringe flowers. A number of these will be covered in the instructions for the Floral Afghan. You no doubt will dream up a few of your own as you develop this skill.

115

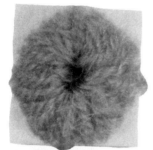

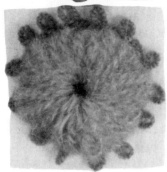

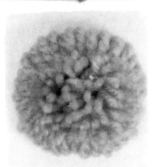

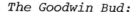

The Goodwin Bud:

The name is rather unusual, but meaningful to those who know the circumstances and the gal it was named for. We are sure that you will use and enjoy this bud with its variations.

Make a few inches of fringe and use a bit of it to stitch a small circle onto fabric as shown for *Fringe Flowers*.

Now thread a tapestry needle with the same yarn and run it through all of the loops. Gather the loops upward by pulling the ends of yarn, then tie the ends, and take them through to the back.

If you wish added detail, use a fine yarn to match or contrast and make a row of flat loops around the edge.

Another interesting variation is made by filling the center with long fringe before gathering the loops. Pull the loops only part way, just until they snug up around the fringe in the center. Now clip the loops to whatever length is desired, leaving them shaggy or clipping close for a sculptured effect.

Another variation was used in one of the large flowers on the floral afghan, and you may wish to refer to that.

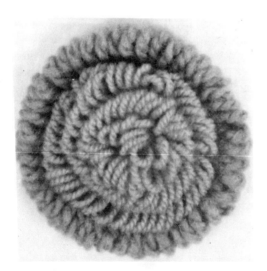

Fringe Flower Centers:

After the fringe is stitched in place to form the flower, a length of contrasting fringe is coiled around to fill the center. The outer edge of the center is stitched first, then the fringe is spiraled inward while holding the loops out of the way with the fingers while the stitching is being done.

If desired, a bit of contrasting yarn could be tucked into the very center for an added touch.

116

Fringe Edging:

In making fringe to edge an item or form a border, consider sewing it to the fabric as it is being made.

To do this, wrap the yarn a few times around the frame and position this on the fabric so that the stitching of the fringe will fall approximately a fourth inch from the edge. Stitch the fringe and the fabric at once. Wrap more yarn onto the frame and stitch, sliding the frame from the loops as it becomes comfortably full.

To turn a corner, plan on rounding it rather than trying to make a perfect angle. Stop about three-fourths inch from the corner. Slip the frame free of all but two loops. Turn the frame a little, wrap and stitch two more loops. Slip the frame free of two loops, turn a bit, add loops, and keep this going until you have completed the corner.

Be sure to pack loops closely as you work on a corner so that the fringe does not become skimpy.

Window Valance
(See Color Section, pattern given.)

This valance was designed to complement our guest room bedspread which is made of the drawings of our six-year-old granddaughters, Shalane and Shannon. (Fabric Crayon idea.) The valance called for simple, childlike figures with lots of variety to match the quilt. Here was a perfect set-up for bringing together a number of designs, yarns and techniques for your benefit as well as ours.

Each and every part of the design is given in the pattern packet. It is suggested that you combine the various items to suit your own needs in decorating pillows, pictures, clothing, etc. If there is a child in your life, you should have great fun with these. You may transfer the designs with a hot iron, or by using the Art Tracing Paper method. (See *Transfer a Design*.)

Valance Construction:
The framework is of 1x6 lumber mounted on angle brackets. The valance is fastened to this with narrow Velcro, one side being stapled to the edge of the board, the other side sewn to the valance edge.

The stitchery design was sketched onto a long strip of butcher paper with the three tallest items being done first. Getting these stitched onto the fabric was the beginning of days of fun as one item suggested another and then another.

When the stitchery was completed, the fringe for the lower edge was made and sewn in place in one operation. (See *Glossary of Yarn Stitches*.) The same size fringe was made in the same way at the hemline of the drapes.

A very narrow fringe was needed for the top of the valance, but it had to be applied after the Velcro was sewn on. This problem was solved by sewing this narrow fringe on bias tape, then gluing it on the last thing.

The finishing of the valance was professionally done at a drapery shop where they laminated it to window shade material and applied the Velcro. It's a good idea to let those with the equipment and know-how help you at these special times. They can usually come up with just the clever ideas to solve your problems.

Before starting with the design instruction, let us emphasize again that in doing yarn work we do not try to duplicate anything. Yarn Stitchery on the machine is an art in its own right, adn we should take pride in making it individual.

All of the techniques used on the valance are described in the Glossary of Yarn Stitches and frequent reference will be made to these.

Stitch the Design:
The grass and small daisies seen on the left are continued across the entire width of the design. Fine yarn was used for these to keep them small and inconspicuous. Grass, stems and leaves are all done in outline, with daisies of lazy daisy stitch and centers of French knots.

In stitching the apple tree, a brown yarn of rather heavy weight was used. Fill-in stitch not only covers the trunk, but is stacked strand upon strand for added thickness in the heavy areas.

The leaves of the tree are also done of fill-in in medium weight yarn. Here the right shade of green was the most important consideration, and most any thickness of yarn would have been alright.

Stems are of fine yarn in dark green, and the fruit is of shiny red yarn coiled high for a definite rounded appearance.

The cat is of grey mohair fill-in, outlined with black yarn of tight twist. White fills the throat area, with bits of green for eyes and pink for ears. Upon completion the mohair was brushed a bit to produce a furry appearance.

The mouse is filled in with dark grey yarn, outlined with black, and the ears are pink.

The cactus is a fill-in of variegated green nylon carpet yarn, a scrap from my collection which filled a need here. The little red blossoms are just bits of yarn stitched into little bumps.

A roadrunner belong near a cactus, and here he is done with lengthwise strands of fill-in. This yarn was too stiff to trail it around the design as we usually do for fill-in. Instead the lengths were stitched, then cut each time at the edge of the design.

The tall daisy is done with rotating flip stitch and the centers are of lifted loops.

Going next to the dragon flies, we find they have wings of shiny blue rayon cord in rotating flip, and the small black wings are fill-in. The slender feelers are outline stitch, and the bodies are fill-in.

The lamb has head and body of fluffy white lifted loops with face and ears of fill-in. Black outlines and details the animal.

This tree needed an irregular, stumpy appearance, and this was obtained by building up the fill-in in some places, and spiraling the yarn to make *knots* in other areas. For the airiness of the willows on the tree, fine yarn of light green was formed into flat loops along the lines, and over this a line of darker green was stitched.

Mr. Skunk was a fun challenge. My yarn collection yielded bits of fine white yarn for the lifted loop stripe on the back and tail. The black part of the body and tail are of mohair, and ears are a bit of grey yarn. A touch of pink makes the collar, with a tiny bit of gold for the eye.

Mushrooms for design purposes may be any color or combination of colors. Warm brown, copper, orange and yellows were used for these to tie in with the over-all color scheme. When doing an item such as this, remember to study the construction of it before you begin stitching. Notice on the large mushroom that the underneath side of the cap has rib-like lines curving up and out from the stem. By simply laying the yarn in that direction as you stitch, you get a natural appearance. The top of the cap gets a heavier yarn of darker color applied *after* the under side is done. Check the smaller items in a similar way.

Peter Rabbit is done with a light grey mohair and fill-in stitch. Notice that each body area is filled in separately. That, plus the fine black outline on the separation lines adds character to the design. The tail is of lifted loops of fine white kinky yarn, and the ears are pale pink. Be sure to brush the mohair for a furry appearance.

The turtle following the rabbit is reminiscent of the tale of *The Tortoise and The Hare*. Stitch the turtle in most any way you wish. This one uses lime green for the head, feet and tail in a fine yarn. The spots are of a variety of yarns, with more concern for color than for texture. The last thing to be done was to outline each area with fine black yarn.

The flowers at the right end of the valance take on tree-like proportions for the sake of balancing the design. The techniques used here are so simple that you will likely adapt them for many uses.

The heavy stems were done first, using a thick yarn of light yellow-green in outline stitch. Next a row of flat loops was made very close to each stem. The leafy items between the stems are of outline, and are simply *space fillers* for balance.

The flowers are of rotating flip stitch in orange, with brown and yellow lifted loop centers.

We find the many items on this valance quite delightful, and hope that you will gain some benefit from the designs and techniques as described here.

Doll Hair

Suggestions for Raggedy Ann and Andy type hair:

Ever sit for hours doing hair by hand on these dolls? No more!
Before you sew the head seams together, sew on the yarn hair. On the
printed commercial pattern instructions you will find that it says to
make three-inch loops on the stamped lines. You can do the same thing
on the machine using the lifted loops between each printed line also.
Start at the top of the head and work your way down to the neck.
Take care to leave the seams free of yarn. Now turn around and work
from the top of the head to the forehead, thus making the bangs lay
toward the face.

You may want to cut the loops for Andy, giving him a mop top
look, and leave the loops for Ann with more of a curled look.

Another fun and easy way to make a full head of hair is to make
it on the fringe frame. (See *Sources*.) The bangs will still be done
with lifted loops as it will look more natural that way.

Floral Afghan
(See Frontispiece, no pattern given.)

The afghan itself is crocheted. The decorated panels are crocheted in *afthan stitch*, which is firm enough to support the load of heavy yarn stitchery. The stitchery was done before the panels were sewn together.

The first step in making the design was to sketch it onto a long strip of butcher paper. Only the stems and the location of flowers and leaves were drawn.

The next step was to duplicate the sketching onto the panels by means of basting with long, galloping stitches. These threads were easy to remove ahead of the embroidery work.

Since the afghan itself is made of acrylic yarns, it seemed logical to use synthetics for the embroidery too. However, the colors and textures of yarn I wanted for the main part were wools from the D.M.C. Company. Their Bulky Wool is so very lovely, and is wonderfully resilient to work with and beautiful forever. And so I shall have this afghan drycleaned rather than launder it.

As to the amounts of yarn needed, a skein of each color was ample, with some left over for another project later. Yarn for the small details was chosen from my collection of this-and-that.

Stems were done first, with some of the leaves being stitched as an extension of the stem.

Flowers came next, and let me explain why flowers of this type were chosen. Ordinarily when doing yarn flowers for pillows, wall hangings, etc., a firm fabric is used, and all the stitches you want to put on it will not hurt it. However, on the crocheted afghan, the objective was to load it with a maximum of decoration while using a minimum of stitching. Therefore, most of the flowers are fashioned of fringe which was made on the fringe frame. In this way the bulk of the stitching is done prior to putting the flowers on the afghan. This same idea would hold true if you were planning to do machine yarn stitchery on a sweater or shawl.

Embroider the Afghan:
A number of different techniques are used in doing the afghan, and instruction will be given for only one item representing each technique.

Tip: Since we will be working with heavy yarn, let us mention again the importance or working with short lengths of yarn. It is difficult to maintain the natural *twist* of the yarn when encumbered with long lengths.

Center Section:

The center section was embroidered first, and an interesting thing caught our eye. The stem was done in thorny stem stitch, and that was planned for all of the panels. However, in considering that the over-all design might look pretty busy with all those jagged lines, it was decided that the stems on the side panels should be done in the twist stitch.

The flower pot was appliqued *after* the stitchery was done. Begin directly on the lower stem, and work it to the top without breaking the yarn. Work in as many of the leaves or leaf stems as you can while you are on the way up.

The lower leaves have a dark stem and vein which were made as the stem was being worked. Afterward a lighter shade of green was worked in a series of out-and-back lines with a flat loop at the tip of each.

The flower nearest the pot is pictured here and shows the outer circle made of wide fringe with loops gathered into petals. The light colored circle is of narrow fringe, and just outside this is a row of flat loops to add a nice touch to the flower.

In the center is a narrow fringe of dark contrast, coiled and stitched as described in the Glossary.

Now let us go to the large flower near the top of the center
section. This was made by first stitching a large circle of wide
orange fringe, which was formed into divided loop petals. (See *Glossary*.)

A circle of wide brown fringe was sewn at the base of these petals,
and this would be later gathered into a spread Goodwin bud. Before
gathering it, however, the center was made of narrow light orange fringe
which was coiled to fill the area. A bit of brown fringe was tucked
into the very center of this.

The last thing done was to gather the circle of brown fringe to
enclose the center. Be sure to have a blunt tapestry or yarn needle
for this work, as a sharp point is difficult to work with for these
hand stitches.

The large bee at the top was made
directly onto the crochet work, and
this became a bit of a problem. So
many stitches cause the threads of
the afghan to spread and buckle just
a little, but it is barely noticable.

The body of the bee is of fine
kinky yarn in lifted loops. The wings
of fill-in stitch are done with finest
mohair in soft yellow, and they look
almost transparent.

Fine black outlines the wings
and makes feelers and legs. Brown
fill-in does the head, with a gold
metallic eye.

While we are doing bugs we
may as well tell about these
other two.

This little fellow has
wings done the same as the
large bee above.

For the body we wanted
gold and brown mixed, and to do
this we used a strand of each
color in a rotating flip stitch.
On reaching the head the two
colors were separated and the
gold was used to form two
protruding eyes. The brown
surrounds the eyes to finish the
head, and the ends of yarn were
then threaded back into the body
and clipped.

The dragonfly was very
simple to do. Wings and feelers
were made the same as on the
others. Body and head are
simply a series of lifted loops
using two strands of yarn.

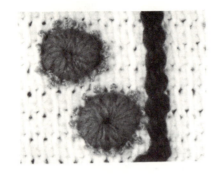

These buds are repeated several times on the afghan, and are shown in the Glossary as *Goodwin Buds*.

These are of fairly fine brown yarn, with fringe made on the smallest frame. After the fringe was stitched and pulled up into the bud, the yarn was tied on the back, and a row of little flat loops of yellow green stitched at the edge.

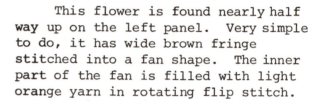

This flower is found nearly half way up on the left panel. Very simple to do, it has wide brown fringe stitched into a fan shape. The inner part of the fan is filled with light orange yarn in rotating flip stitch.

A doubled strand of fine green yarn does the little stem in twist stitch, then the two strands are divided and made into flat loops to form the calyx.

The flower next higher on the stem is made entirely of fringe. The large outside circle is orange and is made on the largest frame. The loops are divided into groups of four to form petals.

A row of medium fringe is stitched at the base of the petals, and this in turn is made into petals centered over the larger ones of the outside circle.

For the center, medium fringe of light orange is coiled and stitched while being closely packed. The loops are then clipped, and if desired may be trimmed for a rounded appearance.

Move to the right panel near the top for this flower. It is made like the flower just described with one exception. The center loops were not clipped, but remain with a bit more bold appearance.

You will find this type of flower so basic and lovely that you will likely think up variations of your own for use on the pretty things you will make.

Variations of this type of flower are to be found on the afghan at top right, lower right, and lower left.

First a length of fringe is made, then stitched into a partial circle or oval.

On this particular flower short lengths of yarn were laid lengthwise on the flower, the center of each length being sewn at the stitching line of the fringe.

Next the yarn laying toward the lower edge of the flower was arranged and stitched even with the edge. Then the upper ends of yarn were brought to the lower edge and carefully arranged, then stitched.

The ends of yarn were trimmed for an attractive fringe. Green yarn was then stitched to form an abstract *calyx* of three flat loops across the lower edge of the flower. Somehow the finished flower looks a bit like an old fashioned girl wearing a bonnet.

You may reverse the procedure in filling the center, having the fringe at the top and the lower edge being smooth and rounded. They were made in this manner on the afghan.

A great deal of love and care has gone into the pages of this book. Many things have been learned and techniques worked out for your benefit and ours.

Whether writing a book or going about our daily affairs, we are constantly scheming to bring new ideas into machine embroidery, and to develop and upgrade existing ones. We hope to continue in making these things available to you.

Good Luck in your pursuit of Creative Machine Embroidery!

Supply Sources

Check your local sewing machine dealers first. They may have the items you need, or might get them. LuRae's, listed below sells to dealers as well as to retail customers.

Following is a list of places to get the supplies referred to in the book.

LuRae's Creative Stitchery
Box 291
Bountiful, Utah, 84010
Phone (801) 292-3292

For a complete list of patterns
and materials for machine embroidery,
ask for a free brochure.

D.M.C. Machine Embroidery Thread
Invisible thread
Machine embroidery hoops
Darning and embroidery springs
Snowflake pattern
Metallic thread
Creative Machine Embroidery, Vols. 1, 2, 3

Bernina Sewing Machine Stores

Mettler Machine Embroidery Thread

Fabric and department stores

Bonded batting